Richie Ashburn Remembered

Fran Zimniuch

Foreword by Harry Kalas

www.SportsPublishingLLC.com

ISBN: 1-58261-897-6

Publishers: Peter L. Bannon and Joseph J. Bannon Sr.
Senior managing editor: Susan M. Moyer
Acquisitions editor: Dean Reinke
Developmental editor: Elisa Bock Laird
Art director: K. Jeffrey Higgerson
Book design: Heidi Norsen
Dust jacket design: Kenneth J. O'Brien
Project manager: Heidi Norsen
Imaging: Dustin Hubbart, Heidi Norsen, Kenneth J. O'Brien
Photo editor: Erin Linden-Levy
Vice president of sales and marketing: Kevin King
Media and promotions managers: Nick Obradovich (regional),
        Randy Fouts (national), Maurey Williamson (print)

Printed in the United States

Sports Publishing L.L.C.
804 North Neil Street
Champaign, IL 61820

Phone: 1-877-424-2665
Fax: 217-363-2073
Web site: www.SportsPublishingLLC.com

This is for Richie Ashburn.
May his life, wit, charm, and
accomplishments never be forgotten.
May I learn to be as good a father
and friend as "His Whiteness."

This is also for Brent, for Kyle, and for Susan.

CONTENTS

FRAN ZIMNIUCH

FOREWORD

Dear Whiteness,

After all those years at the Vet, we have a beautiful new ballpark, Citizen's Bank Park.

Our fans love it, and they especially enjoy strolling on Ashburn Alley, with its shops and restaurants. There are four statues at the new park, Robin Roberts, Steve Carlton, Michael Jack Schmidt, and of course, yours, Pal.

Our fans love this new ballpark so much that we set an all-time attendance record in its first year.

But even with the new ballpark, some things don't change, Pal. Batters still look "hitterish," and base runners still look "runnerish." And there are still pitchers out there that you could, "Go out there right now and get three off." And as always has been the case in baseball, things still happen that are, "Hard to believe, Harry."

Fans frequently mention to me our years together. They haven't forgotten you, and I think about you each and every day, and it is always with a smile on my face and warmth in my heart.

The readers are in for a real treat in this tribute by Fran to a great man and my best friend in life.

I miss you, Pal.

Harry the K

A Bag of Tricks: Richie Ashburn was always in the mood to clown around with his fellow players, like catcher Stan Lopata; broadcasters; family; or listeners. His humor was one of his most endearing qualities.

PREFACE

After visiting beautiful new Citizen's Bank Park in Philadelphia, I was thoroughly impressed with the Phillies' new ballpark. And in this world of corporate sponsorship, the only way to ensure a lasting memorial to the beloved Richie Ashburn was Ashburn Alley. That's why *Richie Ashburn Remembered* came into being. Because for me, Ashburn Alley just wasn't enough.

Surely, by the time a decade or so passes, the odds are that the name of this new field of dreams may change a few times. Just across the street adjacent to the old Spectrum, the Wachovia Center has already had more names than former Phillies pitcher Calvin Coolidge Julius Caesar Tuskahoma "Buster" McLish.

An aging generation of baseball fans remembers Richie Ashburn the ballplayer. Another generation of fans remembers Richie Ashburn the broadcaster, the writer, and the man about town. But there is another generation who will not remember Richie Ashburn the ballplayer or the broadcaster—a younger generation whose only knowledge of Richie Ashburn will be the smiles on the faces and tears in the eyes of fans who miss "His Whiteness" so dearly.

Richie Ashburn Remembered is for all three groups to enjoy. I want those who were lucky enough to see him play to remember just how good a player he was, using his blinding speed and unending competitiveness to only add to his natural Hall of Fame ability. Hopefully, the reminiscing of some of his former teammates and opponents will make that desire turn into reality.

To those who remember the broadcaster, I attempted to capture much of what made Richie Ashburn such a pleasure to listen to during his broadcasts. His knowledge of the game, relaxed approach, and dry wit will never be forgotten by those of us fortunate enough to have heard him. And his Ashburnisms, those favorite sayings and expressions, are still used by many fans today.

And to the younger people who have no idea about why so many of us are so very fond of Richie Ashburn, I want you to understand why.

I saw my first game in the fall of 1963 with my father, who died that winter. But that baseball game, a doubleheader against the Cincinnati Reds, is my fondest memory of him. Before he died, we spoke of seeing more games together. Although that couldn't happen, I found myself smitten by the game. More than anyone else, Richie Ashburn taught me about baseball. His casual, folksy, knowledgeable approach was one that I could relate to easily. After a time, baseball and Richie Ashburn became synonymous. Instead of missing my father because of baseball, I still felt a connection with him through baseball and through Richie Ashburn.

The next season, in what was to be called "the Year of the Blue Snow," by Phillies catcher Gus Triandos, I began to learn the game thanks to Richie Ashburn. Is there anything in life more constant than baseball? If there is, I haven't found it yet. And Richie Ashburn was a constant within that constant.

Richie Ashburn's years in the broadcasting booth made my love affair with baseball real. He taught me not just the game but the nuances of the game. Thanks to "His Whiteness," I have developed a feel for the game that enables me to enjoy America's pastime on many different levels.

The beauty of baseball, its leisurely pace, the strategic planning, and the gut-wrenching moments filled with tension and excitement were brought alive by Richie Ashburn. You knew you could trust him to tell you what was going on at the ballpark. If he was telling stories about Nebraska or sleeping with an old bat (a baseball bat, that is), you knew that there was a lull in the action and that it was okay to go into the kitchen if you needed to. But when his voice rose an octave or two, you knew that it was an important juncture of a game—or sea-son—that should not be missed. Let the pot roast burn, because something big was about to happen.

And those Ashburnisms have stayed with me too and seem to fit like a comfortable glove. To this day, be it a major league game or my son's Babe Ruth League game, when a base runner looks like he's about to attempt to steal a base, the common Ashburn phrase "looking runner-ish" will pop into my head. Or, when a pitcher throws nasty stuff that seems to paralyze a hitter at the plate, I'll hear "His Whiteness" exclaim, "Froze 'em, Andy," in my mind. Or, when a hurler is getting lit up like a Christmas tree, I'll think about my favorite baseball personality say-ing that it was time to "get the married men and the fathers off the field." (Of course, that thought didn't occur much at those aforemen-tioned Babe Ruth League games.)

And so I'd like to thank Richie Ashburn—to thank him for teaching me about the game I love, to thank him for enabling me to love and enjoy it even more because of those lessons, and to thank him for teaching me about aging gracefully, getting the most out of life, and dealing with the loss of loved ones with class and elegance. "Whitey" not only taught me a lot about baseball, but he also showed me a lot about life.

There was a time back in the early 1980s when Richie Ashburn knew me by name because our paths crossed fairly often. And I can tell you what you saw and heard in the broad-casting booth was what you saw and heard in person.

We all miss seeing and hearing from you, "Whitey." *Richie Ashburn Remembered* is for you.

Because Ashburn Alley just wasn't enough.

ACKNOWLEDGMENTS

This project for me is truly a labor of love. I'm fortunate enough to have a number of loves in my life. There are my sons, Brent and Kyle, who I'd do anything for and give anything to. Then there is my beautiful fiancée, Susan, a wonderful gift from God who has renewed my faith in love, relationships, and myself. Finally there is baseball, my first and constant love.

When giving out kudos and thanks for this project meant to memorialize Richie Ashburn, I don't even know where to begin. Phillies Hall of Fame announcer Harry Kalas called "Whitey" his best friend and was his broadcasting partner since Kalas arrived in town from Houston in 1971. His total commitment to helping me with this book is something I'll never forget.

Harry is a class act. I think it's pretty fair to say that Richie Ashburn kept some really good company. In the years since Ashburn's passing, Harry has kept on keeping on. His ability to paint living pictures with his words and melodic voice is a wonderful way to enjoy baseball. But it also seems apparent to me that since losing his best friend, Harry has a sadness in his eyes that was never there before that horrible day in 1997. Everyone deserves to have one friend like Harry Kalas in life. "Whitey" was lucky, too.

Some of his other broadcasting partners and longtime friends were also were kind enough to share their time and stories about Richie Ashburn. Andy Musser, Tim McCarver, and Chris Wheeler gladly spoke about "His Whiteness" and shared many happy memories of their times together. All were an enormous help to me in making this project a reality.

The Ashburn family opened their hearts to me. Richie's sister, Bette, and brother, Bob, gladly reminisced about their brother. His widow, Herbie, and their children—Jean, Sue, Karen, Richard, and John—shared many wonderful memories of "Whitey." Special thanks go out to Richard. Without his patience, confidence, understanding, and belief in my ability to make this book about his father a reality, it never

FRANK LESLIE/FRED McKIE COLLECTION

would have happened. Thank you, Richard. The apple doesn't fall far from the tree.

So many others consented to be interviewed, taking the time to talk about their encounters with Richie Ashburn. No matter who they were or how busy they might have been, there was always time to talk about Richie.

When I spoke with home run king Hank Aaron, you could hear the fondness his heart felt over the phone as he said, "Ah 'Whitey'!" upon hearing Richie Ashburn's name.

The Phillies organization was there for me as well. Bill Giles, David Montgomery, and particularly Larry Shenk went out of their way to work with me as did former owner Ruly Carpenter.

A special thank-you is in order to my cohorts at Sports Publishing L.L.C., particularly John Fishel. His professionalism and support got me through some rough spots in the process. Kudos also go out to my developmental editor, Elisa Bock Laird, who made my manuscript as good as it could be.

The ultimate Ashburn collector, Fred McKie, was also kind enough to share some of his memorabilia. Also, a special word of thanks to the *Philadelphia Daily News*, who allowed me to print excerpts from Richie Ashburn's columns. Former editor Zack Stallberg and sports editor Pat McLoon, along with Paul Vigna and Bob Vetrone Jr., were great to work with on this project. They too were touched by Richie Ashburn and appreciated what he meant to so many people.

Richie Ashburn
Remembered

CHAPTER ONE

THE END

When the Phillies played the New York Mets on Monday, September 8, 1997, no one realized at the time that we'd never hear Richie Ashburn's wonderful voice or enjoy his dry wit again. As each pitch of that meaningless game progressed, Phillies fans all became one pitch closer to losing someone who seemed like a member of the family. That was his final broadcast with the team. His final night.

Ashburn had developed a rapport with fans on the field during his playing days for the Phillies from 1948 to 1959 and on the air after he retired to the Phillies broadcast booth in 1962. His style was all his own. He was personable, winding stories from his childhood in Tilden, Nebraska, into the slower moments of the games the way a grandfather spins yarns about fond times past and that art of storytelling bonded his listeners to him. He would send out special on-air greetings to longtime fans, small children on birthdays, or anyone who was sick. If someone sent some edible goodies up to the booth, he or she would get a heartfelt thank-you over the radio waves. His ability to engage his audience

Lasting Memories: Richie Ashburn's last glove (right) used in his final game as a Mets center fielder.

"Because [Richie Ashburn] did radio and TV for so long, people felt like they had lost a member of their family. Not in my time in the city do I remember a person whose death caused that kind of mourning."

Stan Hochman, *Philadelphia Daily News* writer and columnist complemented his knowledge of baseball. Ashburn had a mind like a steel trap. He combined an instinctual comprehension of the game with his unique sense of humor to make a broadcast enjoyable. It was, to use his words, "a lead-pipe cinch" that fans would be entertained and connected to the action on the field.

A Lead-Pipe Cinch: Ashburn's love for the Phillies and his listeners was a certainty. He connected with Phillies fans on a personal level, making him beloved and irreplaceable.

He wasn't just a ballplayer, a commentator, or an announcer; this 70-year-old former baseball star with his Midwestern drawl and hokey stories about small-town life was a real man, someone Philadelphians could relate to and trust. They knew "Whitey" was there without fail every game, smoking his pipe and chronicling their team.

The Phillies beat the Mets 13-4 that night, which while not remarkable, was certainly unusual for a club mired in last place, 30 games out of first. Even so, the club had been playing well in recent weeks, winning 27 out of 38 games. But this was one of 162 games. Ashburn was even keel about the standings, because the baseball season is a long season and things usually work out in the end, a lesson he undoubtedly learned from his brilliant 15-year Hall of Fame playing career.

He worked his final three-inning stint with Andy Musser on radio that night, and there were no signs that anything was wrong. "Whitey" never bothered to say goodbye. He didn't have to. We'd hear him again tomorrow.

"There was nothing whatsoever that seemed wrong with him," said Ashburn's broadcasting partner and best friend, Harry Kalas. "He was fine. Right up to the end he seemed to be fine. There was nothing leading up to that fateful day in New York. No indication whatsoever. It was just a total shock."

Following the game, Ashburn left Shea Stadium to head back to his hotel, the Grand Hyatt, where the Phillies stayed on road trips to Manhattan. But early on the morning of Tuesday, September 9, at 5:30 a.m., Ashburn called Phillies traveling secretary, Eddie Ferenz, and said he was ill.

"Rich was always afraid that he might die in a hotel room," said his brother, Bob Ashburn. "He just got the idea in his head that it would happen. And ironically, it did."

Ferenz contacted club trainer Jeff Cooper and called hotel security, asking them to send paramedics. They pronounced him dead in his hotel room, No. 1502, at 5:45 a.m. The cause of death was a heart attack.

"I got a call from Jeff Cooper that woke me up at 7:30 that morning," Kalas said. "I just lis-

And Philly Wept: Fans and fellow baseball players mourned the loss of Ashburn after his unexpected death in 1997. Notes and flowers were placed at his plaque on the Phillies' Wall of Fame in Veterans Stadium.

tened to what he said and hung up the phone. Then I called him back to confirm that he had called. He confirmed it.

"It was just like, 'Wow.' I walked around all day in disbelief."

In the last years of his life Ashburn had been slowed by diabetes and some other ailments that were typical for a 70-year-old man, but despite these setbacks he remained active and seemed healthy right up to the end while keeping his diabetes in check.

"It was such a shock," Phillies president David Montgomery said. "'Whitey' gone? It just didn't seem possible. He was so active and vibrant, very athletic—playing squash and tennis. On the road he'd plan some physical activity every day.

"He had battled adult diabetes. He could stop a conversation or a set of tennis and give himself a shot of insulin without missing a beat. But I don't think any of us even had a clue that he was about to die."

Those familiar with diabetes know that the disease can be like a time bomb because those with diabetes have a much greater risk of heart attack and stroke. Although Ashburn seemed to take good care of himself, the disease eventually took a toll on his body.

"I always thought of him taking care of himself physically," said Herbie Ashburn, who had been married to Ashburn since November 1949. "He was an unbelievable athlete. I knew he was having complications from diabetes. When you take insulin, they say your organs age 20 years, so I suppose he had the heart of a 90-year-old. And he had recently developed high blood pressure. But it was just a shock."

THE END

"He had had at least a couple of instances of indigestion that year," broadcasting partner Chris Wheeler said. "He attended a function in Boston that summer and got sick. That may have been a sign now that I look back. My mom died in February of that year, and she had diabetes. She and 'Whitey' used to tell insulin stories about how they controlled their diabetes. They were so funny.

"Jeff Cooper called me early that morning and told me that 'Whitey' had a heart attack and didn't make it. I remember it was one of those times when you just sit straight up in bed."

In the Phillies organization, as the word of Ashburn's death spread, the entire team was affected, on the field and off. Former Phillies owner Ruly Carpenter was on a fishing trip in South Carolina. He had known Richie Ashburn for decades.

"I miss him," Carpenter said. "I'll never forget the morning when I got the bad news. I was fishing, and one of the guys came out to the pond and yelled for me to come in for a phone call. That's never a good thing. It was the Phillies' office, and they told me that Rich had passed away. It was one of the sorriest days of my life. There was no prior warning; it was out of the blue. You were just totally unprepared and it hit you really hard."

Jim Donahue, who had organized the effort to get Ashburn's name back on the Veterans Committee ballot for consideration for the Hall of Fame, was celebrating his anniversary in Cape

A Small Token: This card was handed out to mourners at the Richie Ashburn public service. On the back was a tribute poem by Harry Kalas, which is found on page 9.

May with his wife, Joan. Ashburn was Donahue's boyhood idol and had befriended Donahue during Donahue's tireless but successful pursuit to get Ashburn in Cooperstown.

"The day he died was my [25th] wedding anniversary," he said. "At seven o'clock the phone rang in our room. I knew that wasn't good news. My son told me the news. It was devastating. I had just talked to him the week before. When Richie died, I felt horrible."

Profound sadness and shock were pretty much the reactions of fans all over the Delaware Valley as word spread about Ashburn's death. He had become a comforting presence to those in the area. News of his death really hit home. Many tears were shed all over the region as a favorite adopted son was suddenly gone.

"Because he did radio and TV for so long, people felt like they had lost a member of their family," said veteran *Philadelphia Daily News* writer and columnist Stan Hochman. "Not in my time in the city do I remember a person whose death caused that kind of mourning. He brought back memories of the Whiz Kids and touched many people."

On the Friday following his death, more than 40,000 people, some of whom waited all day, walked past his casket at Memorial Hall at 42nd Street and Parkside Avenue in Philadelphia. Many knelt and prayed. Mourners were given memorial cards with a photo of a young Richie Ashburn on one side and a poem written by Harry Kalas on the other.

"I think the city just sort of adopted him," Herbie said. "They always liked him. He was blonde and handsome and a hard worker. He was very competitive, and they liked that. He also knew how important it was to have good press. Rich was very sincere and he was very cooperative with people.

"He also knew that I was a private person and he did his best to keep the family out of the limelight. You are always in a fish bowl. But he protected us as much as possible."

mayor Ed Rendell," former Phillies chairman Bill Giles said. "We put his coffin at Memorial Hall. In my lifetime in Philadelphia, there has never been that outpouring of grief that we saw because of Richie's passing."

Some of the former players who came to say a final goodbye included Tim McCarver, Larry Christenson, Dick Allen, Garry Maddox, Johnny Callison, Dallas Green, Tug McGraw, Bill Robinson, Greg Gross, Bobby Wine, Randy Ready, John Kruk, and many others. But what stood out was the need for everyday citizens who had never even met Ashburn to pay their respects.

"It was such a shock. 'Whitey' gone? It just didn't seem possible. He was so active and vibrant. ..."

David Montgomery

The funeral, much like Ashburn's life in Philadelphia, was just one more example that illustrated the connection between him and the people in the area that was so deeply felt. Even at a funeral, typically a gathering for the family and close friends, it was different for Richie Ashburn. More than 40,000 ordinary people, most of whom had never met him, felt compelled to attend.

"I came back [from a vacation in Wales] for the funeral and did a eulogy along with former

To realize just how much Richie Ashburn meant to the area, the throngs of people who attended his memorial service gives a good indication of how loved he was.

"That public service in Memorial Hall says a lot," Wheeler said. "For a person to have a place of such magnitude with so many people attending says it all. It was a great loss."

He was a part of Philadelphians' lives. Like a favorite uncle or likeable neighbor, Ashburn had become as much a part of the landscape of the city as the Liberty Bell, Independence Hall, and Billy Penn's statue at the top of City Hall. He was just younger.

With his omnipresent pipe and headgear—be it a baseball cap or stylish fedora, Ashburn was an easily recognizable figure all throughout the Delaware Valley. His charming and folksy Nebraska drawl had become a comfortable sound to Philadelphians for 35 years. Ashburn was an institution in Philadelphia—an icon to those who loved baseball.

"Hard to believe, Harry," he probably would have quipped to Kalas at the grief his passing inspired.

But for those who faithfully followed every intonation of his voice, the hardest part for them was that he was gone.

Unlike many broadcasters who fall head over heels in love with the sound of their own voices, "Whitey" never felt the need to speak unless he had something to say. There were many silent pauses from Richie Ashburn in the broadcasting booth. They were not awkward pauses; they were comforting and expected, adding anticipation for his next comment. But after that Phillies–Mets contest on September 8 ended, the silence from the broadcasting booth became deafening.

"I think a lot of people still miss him," Phillies public relations diretor Larry Shenk said. "But time cures all things, and there will be a day when nobody will know who he was. That's part of life, but it's a shame because he was priceless."

> ## "I think a lot of people still miss him. But time cures all things, and there will be a day when nobody will know who he was. That's part of life, but it's a shame because he was priceless."
>
> Larry Shenk

An Ode To His Whiteness

Harry Kalas wrote a poem for Richie Ashburn to celebrate his 70th birthday. Prior to the first Phillies game following his death, Kalas updated that poem.

His Cornhusker roots have served him well
The dry wit, the humor, you could immediately tell
But the enduring traits we readily see,
His human compassion and love of family
The greatest tribute to an athlete and man
Is that in whatever pursuit, he did the best that he can.
His charitable efforts in memory of Jan
Remind us how fragile is one's life span
Will we ever forget that August in '95
When thousands took that wonderful drive
To Cooperstown, the home of the Hall
An emotional time for us all
When His Whiteness got his just due
We were not surprised because we knew
At Cooperstown on this August day
They honored a man who's a Hall of Famer in every way
When Whitey turned 70, a pipe or hat, I did not send
Rather my lifelong loyalty as a true friend
Now the man all Phillyland loved
Has gone to join Jan in the heavens above
And Don Richie Ashburn by any measure
Was a man whose memory we will forever treasure

"... He was a pesky little ballplayer who you didn't want to see come to the plate. He hit the ball all over, the typical leadoff hitter who also had some power.

"He was very pesky, very annoying to play against. When he got on base, he could upset all your strategy."

Hank Aaron, Hall of Famer

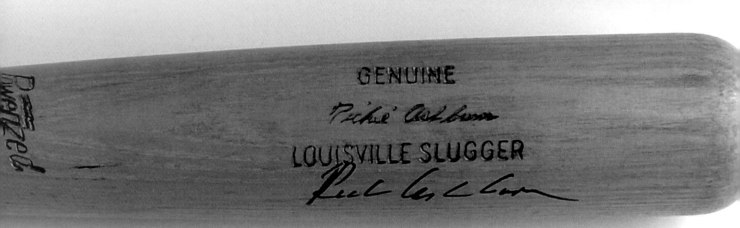

CHAPTER TWO

THE BALLPLAYER

You could take Richie Ashburn out of Nebraska, but you couldn't take the Nebraska out of Richie Ashburn. His roots were firmly implanted in his hometown of Tilden, where he grew up, and his pride in his Midwestern upbringing was the stuff of legend in Philadelphia.

By all of Ashburn's accounts, Tilden was a throwback to a simpler time in America that would probably remind you of black-and-white televisions and apple pies cooling in an open window. It was a tiny town of 1,000 people that didn't even have a stoplight. But everyone knew everyone, and that kind of camaraderie made an impact on Ashburn that was to follow him throughout his playing and broadcasting days in the big leagues.

Batter Up: Richie Ashburn's bat (left), which he used as a player.

The Ashburn family lived in a small house with one bedroom that had an outhouse. It was tight-knit, loving family. Neil and Toots Ashburn were both hard-working people, but they also liked to have some fun. The pair often attended weekend dances at a neighboring town. Married in 1922 while still teenagers, the Ashburns grew up fast. They had two children, Bob and Bette, before being surprised with twins—Don "Richie" and Donna Ruth Ashburn—on March 19, 1927.

The twins were certainly a blessing, but they also added to the responsibilities of the rest of the family. It was not an easy time. Water had to be boiled in buckets, and there were no such thing as Pampers.

"I was five years and two months old when Richie and his twin sister, Donna, were born," said Bette Cram, Ashburn's sister. "Donna cried most of the time, so I was relegated to take care of Richie. It was a pleasure and a joy."

Neil worked in his father's blacksmith shop, bringing home what money he could, but it was during the Great Depression, and money was not plentiful. Christmas gifts were often simple things like a single orange. He later had a successful career in the monument business. Family members have said that Neil was probably even funnier than his second son. The name on his checkbook read, "Neil Ashburn WGB," which stood for World's Greatest Blacksmith.

ASHBURN FAMILY COLLECTION

Doubletake: Ashburn and his twin sister, Donna, surprised Neil and Toots Ashburn on March 19, 1927.

Toots worked as a telephone operator for AT&T and later as a dietician. But no matter how tough times were, Neil and Toots continued to shower the children with love all the while expecting everyone to chip in. As years passed, they often looked with good humor at how they got by in those days.

For example, Toots Ashburn raised chickens, but the family had no money for feed. According to family members she had an ability to know when a chicken was about to die from malnourishment, and so she would send Ashburn with the chicken to the butcher to sell it for nickel.

To add to the meager family income and help put food on the table, Ashburn's dad played second base in a local league for $25 a game—more money than he made in one week at the blacksmith shop.

A Family Business: In the 1920s Neil Ashburn (far right) worked in his family's blacksmith shop. Bob Ashburn, Ashburn's grandfather, is second from the left.

FRED McKIE COLLECTION

But it wasn't all work. The Ashburn children were all very active. As a child, Ashburn played baseball, basketball, and tennis and also swam competitively. He was an outstanding basketball player and probably could have excelled at any sport he chose.

But it seemed that at even an early age that baseball was his sport of choice. Bette remembers the small ghostlike figure of her younger brother darting from tree to tree—Ashburn's makeshift bases—in his nightshirt in the yard after dark. Every evening his mother would find him throwing a tennis ball against the wall and catching it for hours and hours. That love and passion continued to grow as he got older, and his ability on the baseball diamond began to set him apart from other children.

"Richie and I lived in towns 22 miles apart," his longtime friend Fireball Kelly recounted. "We got to know each other by playing against each other in high school and then playing together in the American Legion. …

"Richie was a great athlete. He could have been a great football player, but his father didn't want him to play football because it was a contact sport. His dad knew he was something special. I remember in one American Legion game he hit a single and three pitches later he scored. He stole home before the pitcher even released the ball.

"One time at basketball practice I saw him make 52 free throws in a row. He was unbelievable."

Warming Up: After many attempts to be signed by big league clubs, Tilden's own was spotted by a Phillies scout.

When he was as young as 16, Ashburn had professional scouts drooling and coming to Nebraska to check out Tilden's talented catcher.

"If you've ever been to Tilden, to see that teeny town in the middle of nowhere, it's hard to believe they even found my dad way back then," John Ashburn said.

FRED McKIE COLLECTION

But find him they did, even before they were supposed to. While he was still in high school, at age 16, Ashburn was sent a professional contract in the mail by the Cleveland Indians. Even though he was advised by Neil not to sign it because his father believed it to be illegal, Ashburn's excitement about playing professional baseball got the better of him and he signed on the dotted line.

Shortly thereafter, he and Neil were summoned to the office of baseball commissioner Judge Kenesaw Mountain Landis in Chicago. As he sat in the commissioner's large ornate office with a rug he described as being as thick as the outfield grass, his mouth was dry with anxiety.

Judge Landis voided the contract because baseball frowned on the signing of players who had not yet graduated from high school. Landis fined the Indians $500 to send a warning to other major league clubs. But he took what seemed like a genuine interest in the young catcher and allowed him to keep the $1,000 bonus the Indians gave him.

"The next time I see you, I hope it's in a big league uniform," Landis said to Ashburn as they left his office. (Sadly, Judge Landis never had the opportunity to see Ashburn play Major League Baseball because he passed away in November 1944.)

Following his graduation from high school, the Chicago Cubs came calling and scout Cy Slapnicka signed him to a contract with the Nashville minor league club. But a clause in the contract stated that Ashburn would get a portion of the purchase price if the Cubs bought his contract from Nashville. The clause was illegal, and that contract was also voided, leaving him very disheartened.

Finally, in February 1945, Phillies scout Eddie Krajnik met with Ashburn at Norfolk Junior College and signed him to a contract with the Phillies. He received a $3,500 bonus. This time the contract was legal, and his trek to the big leagues began that summer with the Phillies' farm team in Utica.

The Minor Leagues

Ashburn's professional baseball career began in the Eastern League, with the Utica Blue Sox, where he played under Eddie Sawyer, who would become his future big league manager. Once Sawyer saw Ashburn's speed, he took away what "Whitey" would call the tools of ignorance—his catching gear—and made him a center fielder.

"I remember when he first took off for spring training, he was supposed to be a catcher," said Bob Ashburn, his older brother. "He could really run fast. We all could. Eddie Sawyer switched him to the outfield. My dad thought it was a good idea."

Ashburn joined many of the players, who would go on to become the famed Whiz Kids of the 1950s. In his first year in the minors, "Whitey" hit .312 in 106 games.

Ashburn then missed the 1946 season fulfilling his military obligation. Family members felt that he would head to Korea because of the escalating conflict there; however, when his brother Bob was seriously injured in an automobile accident in San Francisco, the family, including Ashburn, went there to be with him. At that point, the Army stationed "Whitey" in Alaska, where he served as a postmaster for a year and a half. He later would joke with his children that because the day he was drafted into the army was the same day that Japan surrendered, he deserved credit for America winning the war because the enemy had heard he was coming and surrendered.

Returning to baseball in 1947, he hit .362 and led Utica to the Eastern League championship.

"We had a good club and won the Eastern League title," teammate Putsy Caballero said. "Eddie Sawyer made us roommates. 'Whitey' was a helluva ballplayer. The way he could run and hit, you knew he would make it to the majors, barring injuries. With his legs, you knew he would make it. He'd last longer as an outfielder.

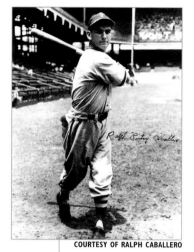

COURTESY OF RALPH CABALLERO

The Roomie: Ralph "Putsy" Caballero met Ashburn in the minors and eventually became Ashburn's roommate.

"Richie was a very nice fellow. In all the time I knew him, I never heard him curse. He was smart and had a good wit. Being a Catholic, I'd go to Mass every Sunday. Richie wasn't Catholic, but this one week he came with me. I told him he couldn't go to communion. But when I got up to the altar, there he was, right behind me.

"We became such close friends. My oldest son was born in Philadelphia in 1949, and I named him after Richie.

The Whiz Kids: Ashburn (far left), Dick Sisler, Del Ennis, manager Eddie Sawyer, Willie "Puddin' Head" Jones, Granny Hamner, Stan Lopata, and Mike Goliot were some of the mainstays of the Phillies teams of the 1950s.

"He was one of the nicest fellows I ever met. You get to have a sense of gratitude to have known him. He really impressed you. He just always fit right in."

When Phillies outfielder Harry "The Hat" Walker held out in a contract dispute after winning the batting title in 1947, it opened the door for Ashburn, who had already opened some eyes with his outstanding season in Utica. He made the Phillies squad in spring training of 1948 and began what was to be a remarkable major league career.

ASHBURN FAMILY COLLECTION

Man About Town: Ashburn took Philadelphia by storm when he was called up to the Phillies.

Big Leagues, Here I Come

Ashburn made it his major league debut in 1948 with some of his fellow Blue Sox teammates—Curt Simmons, Charlie Bicknell, and Robin Roberts. They were all very young—Ashburn 21, Simmons and Bicknell 18, and Roberts 22—so Neil and Toots Ashburn decided it was a good idea to come to the East Coast during baseball season and help the young rookies adjust. They rented a house in Narberth, a Philadelphia suburb, and set up a home for the young turks.

UNITED PRESS INTERNATIONAL

> **I played in the first major league** game I ever saw, on Opening Day of 1948, against the Boston Braves, and the first pitcher I faced, Johnny Sain, was one of the best I would ever come up against in my entire career. Sain had a good fastball and a curveball that exploded through the strike zone. "Son, it's tough to start a major league career against Johnny Sain," Phillies manager Ben Chapman assured me before the game, "but there's one thing about it: You ain't going to face much better after this, no matter how long you play." And he was right.
>
> In my second at bat, I stroked a clean single to center field for my first major league hit. My last major league hit came 15 years later in my last at bat, a single to right field off Bob Buhl. In between there were some disappointments, but for the most part, the memories are wonderful. When you are 21 years old and doing what you always dreamed of doing, how could they be anything else?
>
> **Richie Ashburn's "My 40 Years—A Long Love Affair with Baseball" printed in the *Philadelphia Daily News* on July 15, 1988**

"My mother's cooking is something they still would talk about," Bette said. "My dad was so knowledgeable about baseball that Robin Roberts and the other fellows would sit with my dad and talk about things."

On the field, Ashburn began to show other big leaguers the signs of his fierce competitiveness, especially in the outfield and running the bases where his quickness could make a difference in the outcome of games. His speed, combined with his desire to win, was the first thing that people noticed about the rookie, affectionately called "Ricky" at this point in his career. Whether he sprinted from the dugout to his position in center field or legged out a double from what should have been a single, this innate skill made him invaluable to the Phillies.

"He was one of the quickest from home plate to first base," said Caballero, who spent eight big league seasons with the Phillies. "In 1948, no shortstop could throw him out from the hole. Marty Marion and Pee Wee Reese came close. In our day, we didn't steal as much as you see players do today. If you had 25 steals, it was a helluva lot."

Ashburn stole 32 bases in his rookie season, leading the league. Speed, the one thing in

Dynamic Duo: Pitcher Robin Roberts and Ashburn made their Phillies debuts the same year. Both went on to become leaders of the team.

And They're Off: Ashburn was known for his speed and his humor. Here he demonstrates both at Phillies spring training. The rabbit was provided by photographer Joe Micon who thought Ashburn might perform better against a stuffed opponent.

Fellow Ace: Phillies pitcher Bob Miller was a teammate of Ashburn's.

sports you can't coach, became the signature of his game, and Ashburn used his speed at every opportunity.

"He was one of the fastest guys in the league," said his former teammate and close friend Don Zimmer, a veteran player who later became a major league manager. "Richie was a great bunter, a slap hitter. If he hit the ball to either side of the shortstop, you'd better make a heck of a play to get him out. He was also a great center fielder. He could really go and get the ball. And he was a tough, great competitor. He was like a little dirt bag to play against, stealing a base, laying down a perfect bunt."

"Whitey" was just as solid defensively. His speed gave him the ability to turn a base hit into an out or to force a runner to stop at first when he should have gotten to second base.

"He played hard and was a great defensive outfielder who ran down a lot of mistakes," former Phillies pitcher Bob Miller remembered. "He played as hard as anybody has ever played this game. Running full speed to center field and full speed to the dugout, he gave 100 percent all the time. He ran hard, played hard, and he'd make the great catch. ... He didn't have the power of a Duke Snider, but he set the table for Del Ennis."

Not only did he play the game, he made sure that they game was played fairly. Once during his rookie season when the Phillies were playing the Brooklyn Dodgers, Ashburn helped put an end to the abuse directed at Jackie Robinson from the Phillies dugout. It was

By 1950, Phillies owner Bob Carpenter had surrounded the Whiz Kids with veterans Eddie Waitkus, Bill Nicholson, Ken Heintzleman, Russ Meyer, Blix Donnelly, and Ken Silvestri and added two rookies, Bubba Church and Bob Miller, to the pitching staff. On the last day of the season, Roberts outpitched the Brooklyn Dodgers' Don Newcombe, and the Phillies had their first pennant since 1915 after Dick Sisler hit a three-run home run in the top of the 10th inning. It was the Whiz Kids' last hurrah, but it was without a doubt the happiest moment of my career."

Richie Ashburn's "My 40 Years—A Long Love Affair With Baseball" printed in the *Philadelphia Daily News* on July 15, 1988

Robinson's second year in the big leagues, and he had been a verbal target for many opponents.

"Chapman was a strong opponent of Jackie Robinson playing in the major leagues," Dodgers pitcher Carl Erskine remembered. "Some of the abuse he dealt with not racism, but pure dugout baseball. After Chapman instigated the Phillies to go after him, I understand it was Richie who went to him and said that the more they got on

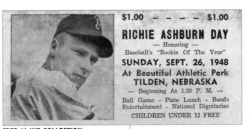

$1.00 — — — $1.00
RICHIE ASHBURN DAY
— Honoring —
Baseball's "Rookie Of The Year"
SUNDAY, SEPT. 26, 1948
At Beautiful Athletic Park
TILDEN, NEBRASKA
— Beginning At 1:30 P. M. —
Ball Game - Plate Lunch - Bands
Entertainment - National Dignitaries
CHILDREN UNDER 12 FREE

FRED McKIE COLLECTION

Tilden's Own: Even after he made the big leagues, Ashburn never forgot his hometown.

[Robinson], the better [Robinson] played."

Ashburn never agreed with the heckling and hatred directed at Robinson.

"Dad had no racist blood in him at all," his son, Richard, recalled. "He loved Jackie Robinson. As a rookie, he was ordered to spike Robinson. It was basically Dad's job, and if he didn't do it, he would have suffered. Players beat on Jackie Robinson every day. Later, Dad apologized to him about it. What

Looking back to the era of the Whiz Kids can be risky for one who sometimes has trouble remembering what happened a week ago, but with the help of my friends, I'll attempt to take you back to "The Way We Were." And as Barbra Streisand sang it so beautifully, "Could it have all been so simple then?"

It was simpler, at least for a while. The nation was adjusting from a wartime economy to peacetime after the end of World War II. You could buy a new Chevrolet for $1,200. And a gallon of gasoline for 18 cents. Major League Baseball was returning to normal with all the good players returning from the armed forces. There were no player agents then, no labor lawyers for the owners to worry about, and the only time you heard the word strike was after a swing and a miss. There was no such thing as a long-term guaranteed contract. Players were paid based on how they produced the year before and nothing else, which eliminated motivation problems. You played well, you got paid well; you played poorly, you suffered.

Richie Ashburn's "The Whiz Kids Baseball, Like The Times, Has Changed" printed in the *Philadelphia Daily News* on April 5, 1983

Fightin' Phils: Ashburn, Curt Simmons, manager Eddie Sawyer, and Willie "Puddin' Head" Jones relax in the dugout during a game.

"He was also a great center fielder. He could really go and get the ball. And he was a tough, great competitor. He was like a little dirt bag to play against, stealing a base, laying down a perfect bunt."

Don Zimmer, former teammate

happened really stuck with him. He knew it was wrong, and it really bothered him. He was deeply ashamed of it."

Ashburn's rookie year was a success. He hit .333, leading the team and coming in second to Stan Musial in the league; was the only rookie elected to the All-Star team; and was named *Sporting News* Rookie of the Year, for his efforts. The Phillies finished sixth in the National League with a 66-88 record.

After the season ended, much like the players, Neil and Toots returned home and picked up with their regular lives in Nebraska.

After his rookie season, things started to pick up for Ashburn and the Phillies; the Phillies finished 1949 in third place with an 81-73 record. In his second season, Ashburn continued to hone the skills that he became known for; he was an avid student of the game and his fellow opponents. This allowed him to capitalize on

First Steal: In one of his first games in the big leagues, Ashburn stole home as it was being protected by Dodger Gil Hodges. Ashburn would lead the National League in steals his rookie year.

opportunities when they presented themselves. For example, he didn't just steal bases because he was fast. He laboriously watched pitchers so he knew whether they were going home with a pitch or they planned to peg the ball to first base to attempt to pick him off.

"Some of these pitchers are pretty cute," Ashburn told Frank Yeutter in a September 1949 interview for *Sports World* magazine. "But even in the short time I've been around, I've discovered a few things. There's a Chicago pitcher who always raises his right heel before he lets go for the plate. If he keeps his foot on the rubber, that's no time to think of running. He's going to try to get me.

"Then there's a pitcher with the Giants who never takes more than one look at first. As soon as he takes that look, then studies the batter, I know he's going to pitch to the plate. Not once last year did he ever take a second look at me, and I stole three bases on him.

"Of course, the right-handers are easier to get started on. Left-handers look right at you,

Why didn't the Whiz Kids win more than one pennant? It is a question we have all asked ourselves many times. Robin Roberts may have had the answer when he declared, "It's not that hard to figure out. We were good, but never quite as good as the teams that beat us after 1950. The Giants put together two great years in 1951 and 1954, much like we put together in 1950. But the Dodgers could have and maybe should have won every year in the early 1950s. Then the best team I've ever seen, the Milwaukee Braves with Hank Aaron and Eddie Mathews, dominated in the late 1950s."

A lot of years have passed since the Whiz Kids played in Connie Mack Stadium, and the times have changed, too. Players used to leave the gloves on the field, and there probably are some major league players around who never rode on a train. And the money certainly has changed. The Whiz Kids payroll for the entire team for the season was $262,000. Mike Schmidt alone will make that much money by the middle of May.

But if times have changed, the game of baseball hasn't. Today's players are trying to do the same things the Whiz Kids tried to do in the 1950s, and that is win. No matter who plays the game and no matter when it is played, you can't ask for more.

Richie Ashburn's "The Whiz Kids Baseball, Like The Times, Has Changed" printed in the *Philadelphia Daily News* on April 5, 1983

and the only way I've discovered to get away is to fool them with body balance. You know— you sorta make them think you're going back to first, but actually you've got the weight on your right foot ready to break as soon as he takes a proper pitching position. That's a pretty tough trick. Learning that balancing stunt and getting a start are the most important parts of stealing."

But that was only the beginning.

The Whiz Kids' Shot at Glory

One of the many highlights of Ashburn's career was the 1950 Whiz Kids team that won the National League pennant, taking on the Yankees in the World Series. "Whitey" hit .303 that year with a league-leading 14 triples.

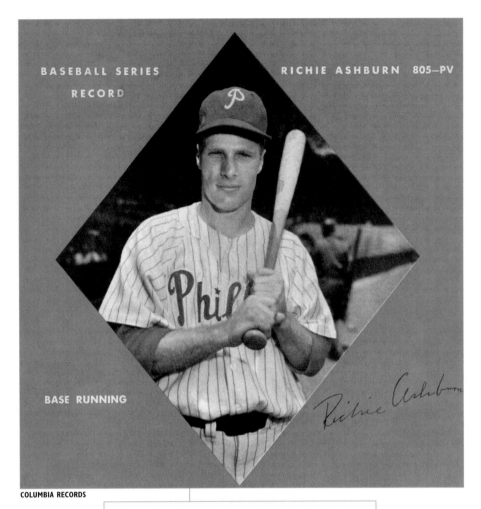

BASEBALL SERIES
RECORD

RICHIE ASHBURN 805—PV

BASE RUNNING

COLUMBIA RECORDS

Recording Genius: Baseball Series made this record for fans to hear Ashburn talk about base running.

He continued to be a team leader, with his solid reputation growing not only on the Phillies, but also around the league.

The final game of the season was a showcase for the Whiz Kids as they went head to head with the powerful Brooklyn Dodgers, who stood between them and a trip with destiny and the World Series. It was a tight game with everything on the line.

The only knock on Ashburn's game was his throwing arm. That one criticism is the ulti-mate irony, because when it counted the most against the Brooklyn Dodgers in the last game of the 1950 season, he made the throw of his life.

"The main criticism on him was his throw-ing arm," veteran *Daily News* sportswriter Stan Hochman said. "They called it a *candy arm.* Yet, he is most famous for throwing out Cal Abrams at the plate to help the Phillies get into the World Series in 1950. It's kind of a mixed message."

The setting was perfect for baseball that first Sunday in October. It was sunny and hot, every seat in Ebbets Field was filled, and Roberts and Don Newcombe were each going for their 20th victory.

They were still going strong in the ninth inning when the Dodgers got runners on first and second with no outs with Snider coming to the plate.

Snider was always a tough out for Roberts, so nobody in the ballpark, at least among the Phillies, expected a bunt.

Snider lined a hard single to center field. I charged the ball and threw a perfect strike to Stan Lopata, and Cal Abrams was out by 10 feet. The play temporarily saved the game but, after intentionally walking [Jackie] Robinson, Roberts still had to retire Carl Furillo and [Gil] Hodges.

My throw to nail Abrams has been cussed and discussed for years. Most of what I've heard has been inaccurate, and some of it has been ridiculous. Some have speculated that Roberts had a pickoff play at second base and that I was playing shallow in order to back up the pickoff attempt. But Roberts didn't have a pickoff play at first base, let alone second.

I've heard I was supposed to be backing up second in case Snider bunted. Totally incorrect. If Snider had bunted when it wasn't expected, the play would have gone to third or first base.

The truth is, I had shortened my position in center field a few steps as every outfielder would do with the winning run on second base in the bottom of the ninth. Snider hit a bullet, a perfect one-hopper, and all I had to do was get off a decent throw to home. To be accurate, it was a fairly routine play executed perfectly in a very crucial situation. If a mistake was made, it was committed by third base coach Milt Stock. If Stock had held Abrams at third, the Dodgers would have had the bases loaded and nobody out, and Roberts would have had to pitch to Robinson, the best clutch hitter in a lineup of great hitters. Stock was fired after the season.

Richie Ashburn's "The Way We Were" printed in the *Philadelphia Daily News* on September 27, 1990

"'Whitey' didn't have a real good outfield arm," Caballero said. "But when he threw out Abrams, it was one of the biggest plays of the year. He threw a perfect strike to Lopata, such a perfect throw that it beat the runner by five or six yards. That got us to the 10th inning when Dick Sisler hit that famous home run.

"Richie kept the 1950 Whiz Kids team alive."

Just 90 miles north of Philadelphia—in Brooklyn—Ashburn's throw to nab Abrams at the plate is not nearly as happy a memory as it is in Philadelphia. But even his opponents admit that it was the most important play of the season.

"One of my strongest memories of Richie is him making the throw at the end of the 1950 season," Dodgers hurler Carl Erskine recalled. "That was the famous or infamous play in Brooklyn. … Ashburn did what a good pro would do. He threw him out at the plate. Must have had him by 10 yards. It was a mistake to try to score him on that play, but Richie took advantage of the mistake.

"We kind of thought that Abrams may have hesitated, but the ball arrived way ahead of the runner."

The Phillies of that season were a close-knit team, and we believed in ourselves. Part of the camaraderie came because quite a few of us grew up together in the Phillies' farm system. And part of it came because, in those days, much of the travel was done by train. It was slower, of course, but it kept teams together off the field. We ate together and socialized together. If we weren't talking baseball, we were playing cards. And those card games could get costly, especially for guys making the $5,000 minimum. Putsy Caballero, the hustler from New Orleans, was the most successful gambler on the team. He claimed he made more money playing cards than baseball. Watching him play both, I believed him.

In one high-stakes poker game in an off-day in Pittsburgh, I won $2,000, a beautiful cashmere sport coat, and a pair of custom-made English leather shoes. The coat and shoes were courtesy of Bill Nicholson, who threw them into the pot when he ran out of money. Before the game ended I lost most of the money, but I still have the shoes.

Richie Ashburn's "The Way We Were" printed in *Philadelphia Daily News* **on September 27, 1990**

We never were able to duplicate that 1950 season even though we were still a pretty good team and usually stayed in the race until September. Perhaps it was because the Phillies waited until 1957 to sign their first black player, while the Dodgers had Newcombe and Robinson, the Giants had Willie Mays and Monte Irvin, [and] the Braves later had Henry Aaron and Bill Bruton.

Or perhaps, like the 1950 Phillies, ours isn't to reason why.

Richie Ashburn's "The Way We Were" printed in the *Philadelphia Daily News* **on September 27, 1990**

"After 15 years of facing [pitchers], you don't really get over them. They're devious. They're the only players in the game allowed to cheat. They throw illegal pitches, and they sneak foreign substances on the ball. They can inflict pain whenever they wish. And, they're the only ones on the diamond who have high ground. That's symbolic. You know what they tell you in a war—'Take the high ground first.'"

Richie Ashburn

Although the Phillies were swept in the Fall Classic by the New York Yankees, they had reached baseball's promised land. The spectacular throw from center field made that date with destiny possible.

"Our Whiz Kids team thought we were going to win again and again and again," Miller said. "But we didn't. I never heard him complain. But I'm sure that not winning again hurt him. We never had any arguments on that team. It was the greatest year of my life.

"There was no doubt about who the leaders on that phenomenal team were. If Roberts was pitching, it was lights out for the other team. Ashburn was there, day in and day out.

"He was the catalyst of that team," Phillies president David Montgomery said. "He was the battler. There was just no way he would ever

No. I For Philly: The Phillies and their fans show their appreciation for their beloved former outfielder.

strike out. He would foul off pitch after pitch until he got one that he liked or drew a walk. He was such a part of that club. Nobody is more synonymous with the Whiz Kids team than Ashburn and Roberts."

Ashburn wanted dearly to make it to the postseason again and to have a different outcome once he got there. But it wasn't meant to be. Although they had some good seasons after 1950, the Phillies never really challenged for the pennant again during his tenure with the team.

"You are with the cream of the crop," his wife, Herbie, said. "Sometimes they make it look easy and it's not easy. That team had Robin Roberts and Curt [Simmons] and Rich.

Juan Marichal was one of the five toughest pitchers I had the dubious privilege of facing in a 15-year major league career. The other four would have been Sandy Koufax, Bob Gibson, Don Drysdale, and an unlikely choice, a left hander by the name of Bob Veale.

Koufax was difficult to hit because of the sheer velocity of his fastball, and he threw a curveball that exploded into the strike zone. Standing up to a 100-mph Koufax fastball and not giving an inch on his sharp-breaking curve took more than a little courage. Fortunately for the hitters, Koufax shared their concern over the possibility of getting hit by the ball.

The same could not be said for Bob Gibson. Gibson had three great pitches, a blazing fastball, a sizzling slider, and a purpose pitch, a pitch used for the purpose of intimidation. You only had to look at the scowl on Gibson's face as he hurtled off the pitching rubber toward home plate. Gibson and I share the same loyalties to the state of Nebraska, but when the game started, I always had the feeling I was standing at home plate dressed as the Grand Dragon of the Klu Klux Klan.

Bob Veale will never reach the Hall of Fame, but he had a Hall of Fame fastball. Veale was a giant of a man who couldn't see very well. Try standing in

CONTINUED ON PAGE 30

Poster Child: Ashburn became a fan favorite in Philly and appeared in a variety of ads for various products.

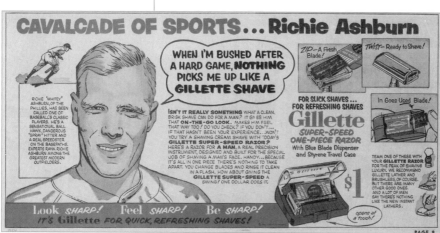

THE GILLETTE COMPANY

RICHIE ASHBURN
OUTFIELD—PHILADELPHIA PHILLIES

FRED McKIE COLLECTION

Pitcher Hater: Ashburn was all business in the batter's box and made sure that the pitcher he was facing knew how little he cared for them.

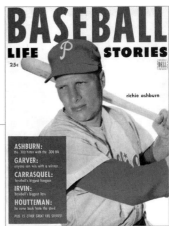

FRED McKIE COLLECTION

CONTINUED FROM PAGE 29

the batter's box against a pitcher who could kill you with his fastball and who doesn't quite know where the hitter is standing.

Marichal had a style all his own, a smooth, high-kick, deceptive delivery followed by any one of five accurately thrown pitches. You could never guess with Marichal. He had excellent control of the fastball, slider, curve, change-up, and screwball. Marichal never was known as a mean pitcher but he would occasionally dust off a hitter if he felt the need...

Marichal claimed I beat him in a game without ever hitting a fair ball. He chuckled and said, "It was a game in Wrigley Field, Chicago, one of those hot afternoons when it's like pitching in a sauna. My manager had told me not to worry about completing the game, just to go as hard as I could for as long as I could. He told me he didn't want me throwing more than 100 pitches because of the heat.

"You were the first batter I faced," Marichal continued. "You worked a 3-2 count, and you must have fouled off the next 25 pitches. I kept throwing strikes, and you kept fouling them off. I almost fainted, and you finally got a base on balls. Here I had thrown around 30 pitches to the first hitter and didn't even get the out. I didn't even get through the inning."

Richie Ashburn's "The Hardest-To-Hit Gang" printed in the *Philadelphia Daily News* on August 2, 1983

"He would have liked to have been there and actually won the World Series."

Although the Phillies of the 1950s never got back to baseball's promised land, the Whiz Kids players continued to be popular in the Delaware Valley. And Richie Ashburn was one of the enduring figures from that magical team.

"He was my idol," Chris Wheeler said. "As little kids, we all liked him. He looked small and could really run and was our favorite player."

Philly's Favorite Son

All throughout his career, Ashburn became and continued to be a popular figure in the Philadelphia area. His feisty style of play and aw-shucks demeanor off the field made him fans by the tens of thousands.

"When I was growing up, I used to have an etching of 'Whitey' sliding into home," Montgomery recalled. "His slides were always feet first, not like you see today. He could take his leg away from the fielder trying to tag him, with a hook slide, or whatever."

That fiery competitive nature made him a force to be reckoned with on the field. He was not afraid to rankle pitchers with catcalls, criticize umpires for questionable calls in the strike zone, or taunt other players from the dugout.

One of the more entertaining aspects of his personality was how he also liked to razz opposing pitchers—a lost art in today's game where players are more sensitive to the taunts. Ashburn was adept at jockeying his way into a pitcher's mind from the bench and intimidating him before he ever stepped into the batter's box. But no matter how hot he may have been, teammates rarely if ever heard Ashburn curse.

"Every pitcher was his enemy," Caballero recalled. "He thought he could get four or five hits in every game. You know, I don't think I ever heard Richie curse. But if a pitcher would get him out, he'd be yelling, 'Judas Priest! You son of a gun, I'll get you next time. How did you ever get me out with the crap you throw?'

"He got along with Roberts and all of our pitchers, but he would really get on the opposing pitchers. He was always a pepper pot, but really well liked."

One time after Milwaukee Braves pitcher Lew Burdette got him to ground out as a result of a nasty spitball, his signature illegal pitch, Ashburn yelled at him all the way to first base, saying that in his next at-bat he'd hit the dry side of the ball.

His distaste for pitchers even went as far as to be included in his home life. At the dinner table, his animosity turned to the good-natured kidding with his daughters.

"It was a family joke," recalled daughter, Jean. "Dad always liked to say that he hoped we would find someone as handsome and funny as he was. And we'd all howl. Then he'd tell us to always remember that he would not have a pitcher as a son-in-law."

But that's not to say that Ashburn didn't appreciate the pitchers who took the art of throwing a baseball to new heights. During his career, he faced some of the best hurlers in the history of the game.

Ashburn studied pitchers throughout his career and became an astute student at the plate, which translated to his success as a leadoff hitter. In 1951, Ashburn led the Phillies in average with .344 and hits with 221 even as team went on to finish 73-81 and fifth in the league.

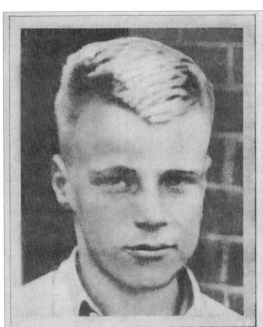

1939—Wheaties Eater! Richie Ashburn at 12 had been eating Wheaties, practicing baseball for seven years. Wheaties and practice —they helped Richie get on his way—earn a berth on the All-American Boy's team. They've been helping him ever since.

1954—Wheaties Champ! Richie's famous for speed. He'll steal a base—beat out your throw to first—rob you of a triple with his speed. Why not? Richie sparks up with Wheaties! They're on his training table several times a week.

The **RICHIE ASHBURN**

Swinging a bat or running the bases, Richie As red-hot spark plug of the Philadelphia Phillies eating Wheaties now for 21 years. He knows—

Champions are MADE, no

Get on your with Wheaties

"Breakfast Cham

GENERAL MILLS

Ashburn's innate competitive nature also translated to his being a daily fixture in the lineup. Fans knew that "Whitey" would have to be very hurt or sick in order to not be at Connie Mack Stadium playing center field. Even when he was sick, he played without any diminished intensity and that earned him the respect of his fellow teammates and other ballplayers.

In one game, Ashburn had a really bad case of the intestinal flu and really wasn't feeling his best. Known to comment often that an illness he was fighting would have left a lesser man in the hospital, this was one game in which he probably should have not played. But in typical "Whitey" fashion, he was on the field and giving it his all.

While going from first to third base on a hit to the outfield, the bug he had got the better of him, causing him to, well, have an accident as he slid into third base.

"Safe!" shouted umpire Ken Burkhart. He took one more look at Ashburn and exclaimed, "Richie, you just crapped your pants!"

Ashburn looked up and replied, "Kenny, that's the best call you've made all year."

Burkhart was not one to be tested and with that remark told Ashburn to hit the showers because he was out of the game. Ashburn ran quickly off the field.

But Ashburn's constant presence on the Phillies made him a team leader and a fixture with the fans. Twice during his career, in 1952 and in 1957, he led the league in games played. Unfortunately, the Whiz Kids always found themselves short of the postseason. From 1952 to 1954, they finished in fourth place with an 87-67, an 83-71, and a 75-79 record, respectively. Ashburn continued to challenge pitchers and patrol center field, but he had developed a reputation for being a difficult player to get out—at the plate or on base.

He was a patient hitter, who had an uncanny ability to hang in there during every at bat, fouling off pitch after pitch after pitch. Even during plate appearances where he failed to get on base, quite often, his efforts at the plate would wear out the opposing pitcher.

"I pitched a lot of innings against the Phillies," Erskine recalled. "I think of how I pitched to him and how I tried to get him out.

Robert R.M. Carpenter Jr. passed away at his home in Delaware last Sunday night. The owner of the Phillies from the mid-1940s until the early 1980s wouldn't have liked the start of this column. To all his family and friends, he was Bob. As far as I know, nobody ever called him Robert, and I know for sure nobody ever called him Junior. For a man who was a millionaire many times over, he was plain and as comfortable as an old shoe. He died as he lived, quietly and without any fuss.

I played 12 years of professional baseball in the Phillies organization while the Carpenter family owned the franchise. Bob was president of the Phillies at a time when there were no agents, no long-term guaranteed contracts and no such thing as free agency. It was a time of the reserve clause, which bound a player to one team forever. In other words, a player's welfare depended pretty much on the mercy and fairness of the owner. And Bob Carpenter was fair with his players to a fault.

Bob was a pussycat when it came to negotiating contracts, especially if the player had a family. And if the player and his wife had a new baby during the offseason, that usually was good for an extra $5,000, no matter what kind of season the player had.

Bob personally loaned me $15,000, interest free, to build my home in Nebraska. And I know for a fact he did the same thing for Willie "Puddin' Head" Jones and Granny Hamner when they bought homes. And when

CONTINUED ON PAGE 34

The best we could do was pitch him with high fastballs away and hope he'd hit liners to the left fielder. He always made contact, like Stan Musial. He always got his bat on the ball. I once threw him nine straight 3-2 pitches in a game in Philly, and he fouled off eight of them.

"He was a pure leadoff hitter, and he had that mentality. His on-base percentage was more important than hitting for power. That was his forte. He had speed and a good eye at the plate. He did not strike out much, and he got a lot of walks."

The likes of Willie Mays, Duke Snider, Mickey Mantle, Stan Musial, and others hit with more power and got most of the press clippings. As they spent their career with more successful teams and received more widespread attention from national scribes, Ashburn quietly went about his business, day in and day out, as one of the best hitters of his era.

"He was probably as good a leadoff man as you'll ever see as a ballplayer," Roberts posited. "He is definitely a guy who you can compare with players like Mays, Snider, and Mantle."

In 1955, Ashburn won his first National League batting title with an average of .338, beating out great hitters like Mays, Musial, Roy Campanella, and Aaron. Although he certain-

ly took personal pride in the accomplishment, Ashburn was still the consummate team player who was more interested in winning baseball games than awards.

"I knew him more as a broadcaster than opposing him as a player," Hall of Famer Hank Aaron said, "but I did play against him. He was a pesky little ballplayer who you didn't want to

RICHIE ASHBURN

FRED McKIE COLLECTION

see come to the plate. He hit the ball all over, the typical leadoff hitter who also had some power.

"He was very pesky, very annoying to play against. When he got on base, he could upset all your strategy."

Of his many attributes as a baseball player, Ashburn had the uncanny ability to spoil pitches that he didn't like that were strikes by fouling them off into the stands. Oftentimes, he would frustrate opposing pitchers by fouling off pitch after pitch, which would lead on many occasions to a hit or a base on balls.

When the Phillies played the New York Giants on August 17, 1957, "Whitey" took this foul balling art to new levels. An unfortunate spectator that day, Alice Roth, the wife of

CONTINUED FROM PAGE 33

Hamner fell into some hard times at the end of his playing career, Carpenter gave Granny a job in the organization.

I know Bob was responsible for helping the families of three of his former players who ran into financial problems after they retired. I know of at least two children of his former players who completed college due to his generosity, and I'm sure there were many others.

Bob Carpenter wasn't the perfect owner. He waited too long to actively scout and sign black ballplayers. On the other hand, Dick Allen, the best black player the Phillies signed, loved Bob Carpenter. When Allen was told of Bob's death, Allen said: "He was like a father to me. There is nothing I would not have done for Bob Carpenter."

At contract time, he always said to me half-jokingly, "Why couldn't you have been Duke Snider or Willie Mays?" I talked to Bob for the last time in the summer of 1987 at Veterans Stadium. He was fighting the cancer then.

Always a big, strong bull of a man, he was noticeably thinner and weaker that night. He hugged me and said, "You didn't have to be Snider or Mays for me. You did just fine."

Richie Ashburn's "As Owners Go, 'Bob' Was One In A Million" printed in the *Philadelphia Daily News* on July 11, 1990

Philadelphia Bulletin sports editor Earl Roth, could speak to Ashburn's ability to send pitch after pitch into the stands.

That August afternoon, he hit Mrs. Roth twice during the same at-bat.

The first foul ball hit her in the face, breaking her nose. Medical personnel attended to her and placed the injured woman on a stretcher. As she was receiving help, Ashburn continued to foul off pitch after pitch. As Mrs. Roth was being removed from her seat on the stretcher, Ashburn hit her with another foul ball.

Ashburn's knowledge of the strike zone also made him very pesky for umpires to deal with at times. "Whitey" would give them a hard time if he thought their calls were off. In one particular game in Milwaukee, umpire Jocko Conlan got tired of "Whitey" giving him lip about how he called balls and strikes. Ashburn recalled the story in a 1989 column for the *Philadelphia Daily News:*

"After griping on a couple of calls in Milwaukee, Jocko said to me while I was at bat, 'You little blankety-blank, I'm getting tired of hearing you bitch. Let's see how good you can call 'em. You call your own pitches in this at-bat.'

"The Braves catcher, Del Crandall, said, 'You've gotta be kidding.'

"I said, I know I can do a better job than you're doing, Jocko.'

"Jocko said, 'Play ball.'

"Now I had a problem. I had to worry about getting a hit and calling the pitches. And most important, I wanted to show Jocko I knew the strikes from the balls. The first pitch was probably low, but not wanting to take advantage of the situation, I called it a strike. The sec-ond pitch, I flat-out blew. The ball bounced into Crandall's mitt and I called it strike two.

"I looked back and Crandall was laughing. So was Jocko.

"'You are probably the first hitter in the history of the major leagues to have the opportunity to call his own pitches and you missed them both,' Jocko said with haughty grandeur. 'I may be horsebleep, but you're worse than I am. I'll call the pitches.'"

Although Conlan gave Ashburn a lesson in calling pitches and the strike zone that day, Ashburn continued to succeed at the plate. In 1958, the Phillies were way out of contention—they ended the season in eighth place with a 69-85 record, but the only drama left was to find out who would win the batting title, Ashburn or Mays, after each player finished their final game of the season. Both outfielders stayed in their games until the last out. Ashburn's final game saw the Phillies defeat the Pirates 6-4 in 10 innings. In Pittsburgh, Ashburn went three for four, increasing his average to .3495. Later that day in the Giants' victory over the St. Louis Cardinals, Mays went three for five to finish the year with a batting average of .3466. Ashburn's average was rounded off to .350, and he clinched his second batting crown.

"He wasn't much of a home run threat, but we faced the Phillies 15 or 20 times a season, and he was a tremendous player," Hall of Famer Willie Mays said. "He hit .300 [consistently] and beat me out for the batting title a couple of times. In 1958 he beat me out by a couple points. I think the last game of the season I went three for four, but he went four for four. He got some bunt base hits. I called him up and kidded him about it."

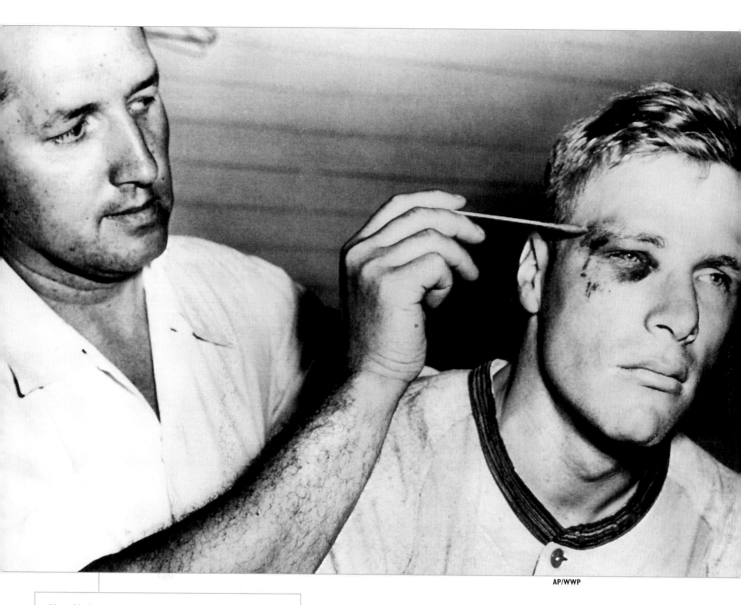

AP/WWP

No Sick Days: Ashburn's intensity on the field meant that he missed very few games due to illness or injury.

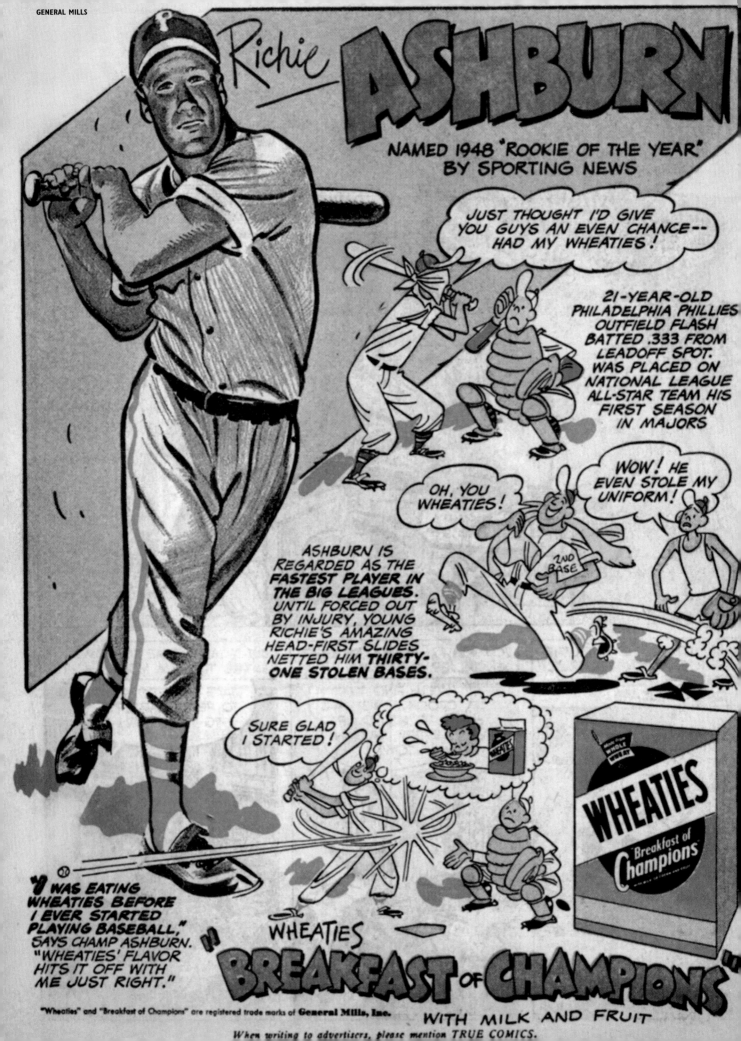

In spite of his success, the 1950s were still a time when it was difficult for players to share the wealth with the owners. Hard as it is to believe, winning a batting title didn't necessarily mean a jump in salary. A decade before, Harry Walker opened the major league door for Ashburn by holding out for a raise after winning a batting crown. The owners held all of the cards because the reserve clause was in place, which tied a player to his club for life. As many players discovered before and after, a great successful season didn't necessarily mean more money. The experience left a sour taste in Ashburn's mouth.

In 1959, the Whiz Kids continued to struggle and Ashburn's production fell off. In his final season with the Phillies, he hit a career-low .266, garnering a career-low 150 hits as a regular player. That's when there were rumors that his time with the Phillies could be close to an end.

"My first assignment at the *Philadelphia Daily News* was on June 10, 1959, when Larry Merchant, the sports editor, asked me to call Ashburn to talk about some trade rumors," veteran *Daily News* sportswriter Stan Hochman said. "He was a very good interview. He told me that if he had to leave that he'd like to go to Chicago, where the Cubs played all day games."

After 12 seasons with the Phillies, Ashburn was traded to the Chicago Cubs in January 1960 in exchange for John Buzhardt, Alvin Dark, and Jim Woods. Rumors had spread for a while about a possible trade. Although it's always a shock, there was little a ballplayer could do to dictate his destiny.

"He just accepted it," his wife, Herbie, said. "Twelve years in one place was not the norm.

He was just grateful he got to stay in one place for so long."

Even after Ashburn left the Phillies, he remembered the city, the fans, and the organization fondly.

Chicago and New York Bound

Ashburn rebounded nicely in Chicago, hitting .291 in 151 games for the 1960 Cubs.

"He only knew one way to play," teammate Don Zimmer said. "He was the type of guy who always played hard. He just kept digging."

Ashburn also enjoyed the same congeniality he had with his Phillies teammates in Chicago. He would joke around with his teammates in the clubhouse and the dugout. For example, in a story Ashburn swore was true to former Phillies chairman Bill Giles, before a game one day, Cubs pitcher Jim Brewer came up to Ashburn, knowing Ashburn's amazing skill for hitting foul balls, and asked for a favor. Apparently Brewer had been having some marital problems, and he knew his wife was going to be at the ballpark for the game. Brewer asked Ashburn if the leadoff man could foul a pitch off and hit her with the ball. During the game Ashburn came up to bat and coincidentally knocked it about one or two feet away from her. Without waiting for the next pitch, Brewer stuck his head out of the dugout and yelled at Ashburn, "Two feet to the right and you've got her."

During Ashburn's tenure with the Cubs, Chicago management also tried an innovative, if unsuccessful, new idea—a group of coaches who took turns as manager. It was known as the College of Coaches. The idea failed miserably.

"It was like a circus," Zimmer said. "Like a popularity contest. One guy had about seven or eight games, then he'd go to Houston, which was our Triple-A team. Then they'd bring in another guy. The first three coaches they brought in, I played regularly for. Then, the fourth one, I never played."

Following that example of a failed baseball management experiment and another sub-par campaign in which he hit just .257 in 109 games in 1961, he was made available in the expansion draft that would supply players for the two new National League teams, the Houston Colt 45's and the New York Mets.

The Mets chose Ashburn as well as some other players such as Marv Thornberry, Frank

BRACE PHOTO

One of the Guys: Rod Kanehl played with Ashburn toward the end of Ashburn's career.

Thomas, Clarence "Choo Choo" Coleman, Jay Hook, Roger Craig, Zimmer, and a host of others. That Mets squad would be managed by legendary skipper Casey Stengel.

"Richie was just one of the guys," teammate Rod Kanehl recalled. "But he also kind of kept to himself. He had no problem with anyone on that team. He and Casey always got along great. They both knew how the game should be played. Casey didn't put a lot of pressure on us. He knew we didn't have any pitching. Richie and Casey used to reminisce about the 1950 World Series a lot together."

That Mets team still holds the major league record for futility with a record of 40-120.

I got a taste of it [no financial reward] in 1958, after hitting .350 and beating out Willie Mays for the batting title on the last day of the season. The Phillies sent me a contract for a $2,500 cut, explaining, "You didn't hit your singles far enough."

To which I responded, "If I hit them any farther, they would be outs."

That's the way it used to be. But however bad it was, there must have been a lot of good. DiMaggio, Slaughter, Ennis, Callison, Nicholson, Walker, and I all agreed that it was the best time of our lives.

Richie Ashburn's "Unkindest Cuts For Old-Timers, Great Years Didn't Mean Great Salaries" printed in the *Philadelphia Daily News* on April 9, 1990

Still Swingin': Ashburn warms up prior to a game at Wrigley Field. After 12 years with the Phillies, he was traded to the Cubs in 1960.

They just weren't very good and no matter how the team tried to solve its problems, the losses kept piling up.

For example, Mets shortstop Elio Chacon, who was from Venezuela, made 22 errors that season and kept getting in Ashburn's way. Every time a ball was hit to short left-center field, Ashburn would yell, "I got it! I got it!" but the 160-pound Chacon, who was also trying to make the catch, would run into him. Finally, they figured out the problem. Chacon didn't speak any English and therefore, didn't realize Ashburn was calling him off the ball.

Ever the innovator and never too old to learn something new, the veteran Ashburn learned how to say "I got it" in Spanish—"Yo la tengo." Now that they had solved the language barrier, Ashburn assumed nothing could go wrong.

The next time a ball was hit between Chacon and him, Ashburn yelled, "Yo la tengo! Yo la tengo!" He was delighted to see Chacon

Phil Wrigley was one of the wealthiest men in the country, and as president of the Wrigley [chewing gum] Corp. and owner of the Chicago Cubs, he could afford to be a little eccentric. Maybe it was an idea that was ahead of its time, or maybe the idea never had a time. Whatever, it was an idea that didn't work very well...

Mr. Wrigley, with the help of his general manager, John Holland, hired Bobby Adams, Dick Cole, Rip Collins, Harry Craft, Charlie Grimm, Vedie Himsl, Gordie Holt, Lou Klein, Fred Martin, Elvin Tappe, and Verlon Walker as his coaches. All were associated with baseball, but only two, Grimm and Craft, had managing experience.

Indeed, the first designated acting-manager has become a trivia question. Vedie Himsl was the first. Himsl was a decent sort, but his baseball experience came from working in the Cubs' accounting department.

Himsl won 10 and lost 21. During his tenure, reliever Don Elston won three games and saved one. Elston, living in Chicago, recalled, "It was Mr. Wrigley's idea, so we had to live with it. But when one guy was head coach, he didn't get much help. There was a lot of jealousy among the coaches who were just sitting around waiting for their turn to manage."

CONTINUED ON PAGE 45

back off. He relaxed, settled under the ball, and was ready to make the catch—until he was run over by 200-pound left fielder Frank Thomas, who spoke no Spanish.

"Richie was a special person," Zimmer said. "'Whitey' hit .306, and then he quit. He retired. Not many guys hit .306 and retire. He was tired of losing and didn't want to go back to another losing season."

Ashburn's .306 average in 135 games led the Mets in hitting, but it was a frustrating experi-ence for any professional athlete to be mired on a team that simply couldn't win many games. On the last day of the 1962 season, Ashburn played in his last professional game.

"In Richie's last play in the big league, he was the third out of a triple play," Kanehl recounted. "Joe Pignitano hit a blooper against the Cubs over the head of Kenny Hubbs. But Hubbs caught the ball, threw out Sammy Drake at second, and then Ashburn was out at first even though he made a beautiful pop-up slide.

He went right into the dugout and on his way to the clubhouse he said, 'Boys, that's a fine fucking way to finish this year. See you next year.'

"Then he went into the clubhouse, and we never saw him after the game. I think he had enough. …

"He was the most competitive player I ever played with," Kanehl said. "When he put his uniform on, he was all business. Even with the Mets in 1962, his last year, he just went out there every day and ran every ball out. He even hit .300. Pete Rose didn't have anything on Richie. He was every bit the hustling player as Rose."

Ashburn's accomplishments on the field spoke for themselves. That ability coupled with his engaging personality made him a popular baseball person throughout the league. He had a wonderful ability to poke fun at himself and others.

The Class of 1961: Ashburn (second from left) joins potential Cubs outfielders at spring training. With him are Al Heist, Bob Will, Lou Johnson, Danny Murphy, Billy Williams, and George Altman.

AP/WWP

Still Smilin': Ashburn, Al Jackson, Rod Kanehl, and Charlie Neal were all a part of the 1962 Mets—the worst team in baseball history.

"I knew him as a player some but much better as a broadcaster," said Larry Dierker, a former pitcher with the Astros and St. Louis Cardinals and later an Astros manager. "He used to kid me about writing a column like he did. 'Whitey' used to say that we were the only former ballplayers who were smart enough to write and be broadcasters at the same time.

"After getting to know him a little bit, I took a look at his offensive accomplishments. I was really glad he got into the Hall of Fame because he certainly deserved it. He played at a time when there were a lot of great center fielders who hit with power and drove in a lot of runs. That was not his role. He was the best leadoff man in the business in his time. There are 20 or 30 teams in Major League Baseball who would give anything to have a guy like him leading off right now.

"Good hitters like 'Whitey' who didn't have power don't get the credit they deserve. He used to tell me that in spite of the great outfielders of his time that he almost always led the league in total chances. That's a great indicator of range, which is the most important factor for a center fielder."

At the end of his career, Ashburn garnered 1,875 hits in the decade of the 1950s, more hits than anyone else from that era. That list includes players such as Nellie Fox, Stan Musial, Alvin Dark, Duke Snider, Gus Bell, Minnie Minoso, Red Schoendienst, Yogi Berra, and Gil Hodges. He won two batting titles and led the league in several categories. But no matter how successful he was, he never let it go to his head.

"Richie was the same guy at the start as he was at the end," said Fireball Kelly, his best friend for 54 years. "Just a fantastic guy. He just did not have the ability to tell anyone, 'No.' He'd sign autographs for hours after a game. I honestly don't think another baseball player signed as many autographs as Rich."

CONTINUED FROM PAGE 42

And that is why Mr. Wrigley's plan backfired. His intention of eliminating pressure on a manager actually triggered a competitiveness among the coaches that created havoc on the ball club. Stability is very important to any team, and when you have a situation in which each coach has his own ideas on a lineup [and] his own ideas on hitting, pitching, fielding, and the strategy used in a game, it can get very confusing to the players.

A worst-case example would have been Lou Brock. Unfortunately for Brock, he joined the Cubs as a 21-year-old rookie at the same time Mr. Wrigley installed the College of Coaches system. Brock was an outstanding raw talent, but if he were to develop into a great player, he needed instruction. Brock got instruction, all right. A very talented and confused Brock got traded to the St. Louis Cardinals in 1964 for pitcher Ernie Broglio. He got 11 different ways to hit, field, and run the bases. Brock went on to the Hall of Fame, and Broglio only won seven games for the Cubs in three years...

But the College of Coaches was a total failure for major leaguers, and Mr. Wrigley's grand management design was abandoned after two seasons. It took him that long to discover what his players suspected all along, that the only thing worse than one bad manager is 11 bad managers.

Richie Ashburn's "Recalling the College of Coaches" printed in the *Philadelphia Daily News* on December 23, 1986

CHAPTER THREE

THE BROADCASTER

"The word to describe 'Whitey' is charming.

He just had an innate ability to charm people. ...

He always made you smile and then turned the

smile into a laugh. He wasn't bashful and he

framed issues differently from most of us.

You just related so well to him. You wanted to

hear his stories. Did you hear them before? Yes.

Did that matter? No. Listening to 'Whitey' was

like enjoying a great song or piece of music."

David Montgomery, Phillies president

Bobbin' Along in the Booth: Ashburn took his knowledge of the game from his time as a player and shared it on the air when he became a Phillies broadcaster.

"Boys, this game looks a lot easier from up here."

Richie Ashburn,
in the broadcasting booth

I wish I would have been getting paid by the mile. At the end of this season—my 25th as a Phillies broadcaster—I will have logged, give or take a few miles, close to one million miles on airplanes and buses watching the boys of summer play baseball. As one of my old farmer friends in Nebraska would say, "That's a lot of wagon greasin's."

I had retired to the state of Nebraska when I was offered the job as color commentator for the Phillies games at the end of the 1962 season. Having played my 15th and last major league season with the 1962 Mets—who, on merit, were the worst team in the history of the Grand Old Game—I had had enough of playing and had very little stomach for staying in the game as a coach or manager.

Being part of a team that loses 120 games in one season can do that to you.

CONTINUED ON PAGE 50

R ichie Ashburn always felt that had he not gone into broadcasting at the end of his outstanding baseball career, that he would have been elected to the U.S. Senate from the state of Nebraska. That may or may not have been the case, but the Cornhusker State's loss was most definitely the gain of sports fans in the Philadelphia area.

In 1963 "Whitey" climbed into the broadcast booth at Connie Mack Stadium with By Saam and Bill Campbell to begin what would become his second career as a color man for local radio and television. The fan favorite of the Whiz Kids immediately developed an intimate relationship with Phillies fans, who felt like they were listening to a trusted old friend right in their living rooms.

"His delivery on air and sense of humor came across readily in the booth," Phillies chairman Bill Giles said. "People loved it. The way he delivered things was casual and informed. He kind of winged it."

A Style All His Own

Just why "Whitey" was so popular and revered as an announcer is difficult to explain. If you were to compare his style to Broadcasting 101, he did not fit the mold of the typical color

FRED McKIE COLLECTION

Mike Mates: Early in Ashburn's (center) broadcast career, he was joined in the booth by Bill Campbell (left) and the great Bryum Saam (right).

"When the game starts, my job begins."

Richie Ashburn

CONTINUED FROM PAGE 48

I could have played at least another season, maybe more. The Mets general manager, George Weiss, offered me a $10,000 raise—which was generous by 1962 standards—but I had made my decision to retire. I wrote to thank him. In the letter I noted, "I wouldn't have missed the 1962 season for anything but I wouldn't want to go through it again." A few days later, I wrote the required letter to the National League office to officially announce my retirement. ...

My first reaction was to turn the [Phillies announcing] job down—and I did. ...After the holidays, that was always the time of year I started getting the itch to start baseball again, and this year was no different. I found I wasn't ready to walk away from the game I loved so much. I wouldn't be on the field. I wouldn't be involved in wins and losses, and I felt I would miss the competition. I knew how I felt about the game as a player but had no idea how I would feel as a spectator.

It took a while, probably a couple of years, but I discovered I didn't need winners and losers to enjoy the game of baseball. It's nice if the team you're working with wins most of the time, but losing doesn't necessarily detract from the quality of play. A clutch hit, a brilliant defensive play, a great throw, a double play—whatever it takes at the moment—are not always accomplished by the winners.

Rich Ashburn's "Hard to Believe, Harry—Rich Ashburn Entering 25th Year as Phillies Broadcaster" printed in the Philadelphia Daily News on April 7, 1987

commentator. Ashburn would weave in stories from his youth in Nebraska, and he would talk to listeners like he would talk to a person on the street. His style was down home and friendly. Fans who tuned in to the games felt like Ashburn was right there in their living rooms. He wished faithful followers happy birthday on the air or sent out personal greetings. That could have been the reason for his success. Ashburn was just being Ashburn. He was no different in the booth than he was as a man.

"When I first joined the Phillies in 1971, Richie took me under his wing and made me feel welcomed in Philadelphia and with the Phillies," Harry Kalas recalled. "He had such a great knowledge of the game and had the expe-

rience as a Hall of Fame player. He understood the nuances of the game. ... 'Whitey' was a superb color analyst.

"As he told me, if he didn't have anything to say, he was not going to say anything. There would be periods of time when there was not a lot of chatter until he had something worthwhile to say."

A broadcaster's worst fear is dead air, so standard procedure is to keep talking. Ashburn bucked that trend. If he had something to say, he said it. Fortunately, for Phillies listeners,

Fun-Philled Voices: Chris Wheeler, Andy Musser, Harry Kalas, and Ashburn made up the Phillies broadcast team in the 1990s.

PHILLIES BROADCASTERS

PHILADELPHIA PHILLIES

Ashburn had a lot of personal stories that would come to mind as he watched the game.

For example, during a spring training exhibition game in Florida from Kalas's first year on the Phillies broadcasting team, he and Ashburn watched as a player broke his bat to hit a foul ball.

While the player went to get another bat, Kalas said, "Rich, the game bat must be very important to you."

"It really is, Harry," Ashburn said with a straight face. "In fact, when I was playing and going well with a certain bat, I would not trust leaving it around the dugout or in the clubhouse. I used to take it back to my room and go to bed with it.

"In fact, I've been in bed with a lot of old bats in my day."

His success in commentary was known even outside of Philadelphia, and some even encouraged him to stay away from doing play-by-play so that listeners could get more of the Ashburn persona during breaks in the action and between batters. When Gene Kirby arrived in Philadelphia in 1971, he was put in charge of the Phillies' radio and TV operation. Kirby had heard Ashburn's commentary when Kirby was working in Montreal and so he set up a lunch date with the former Phillies ballplayer to talk to him about the broadcasts.

"I told him that he did a great job, but I felt that he should confine his activity to doing the color, not play-by-play," Kirby remembered. "You should have heard him, 'I only do one inning of play-by-play. You might as well cut off my arm.'

"He did such a great job we wound up giving him three innings of play-by-play.

"Rich was completely honest. Everything he said had a meaning to it. There was not a lot of strategy, which he knew so well. He told the people what was really happening. There was nothing put on about him, and he always had a smile on his face. The fans loved him; they really did."

His straightforward approach to the game was also reflected in his broadcasts. In baseball there are slower periods between the action on the field that can be filled with insights about the team or engaging stories told by the broadcaster. Ashburn had a knack for both.

"He reached out to the community and was very accomplished. He was fun on the air and had a nice slant on things," broadcasting partner Andy Musser recalled. "Baseball is a daily soap opera during the summer. Unlike hockey, basketball, or football, there is a lot of time between the action, which the announcers need to fill. You are with us on a daily basis and you get to know us. There is so much free time

"Right down the middle for a ball."

Richie Ashburn, criticizing an umpire's call

on the air that the real person comes out. You can't fake it. People felt like they knew him."

For example, during another game, the Phillies announcers brought up the new tradition of the ballpark's organist playing a tune as each batter stepped into the batter's box. Although it wasn't done when Ashburn played, the former center fielder was asked what song they would have played for him.

Without missing a beat, he replied, "Mr. Wonderful."

"It was just he way he presented himself that made him so special," former Phillies owner Ruly Carpenter explained. "His Midwest low-key manner. But he always came through with funny and insightful remarks about the game and how it was supposed to be played."

Even Carpenter was not above being a target for Ashburn's jesting—well, sort of. According to former booth pal Chris Wheeler, he and "Whitey" were covering a Phillies game on television in late September when Ashburn made a shocking announcement.

"We'd like to send our best along to former Phillies owner Ruly Carpenter," Ashburn said. "Ruly was involved in a car accident today. ... We hear he's doing OK."

Wheeler was stunned by the news because he hadn't heard anything about the accident, but he figured that Ashburn had heard about it from one of his connections.

Ashburn continued to tell a story on the air about how the Carpenters still owed him $500 from the 1950s, how the bill with interest would be around $50,000 by now, but he knew he would continue to wait for payment because the family was cheap—this was an ongoing joke between Ashburn and Carpenter.

At the end of the inning Phillies publicist Larry Shenk came down the stairs with a puzzled look on his face.

"'Whitey,' where did you hear about Ruly being in a car accident?" he asked.

"Well, some guy I had dinner with in the pressroom tonight told me."

"'Whitey,' you had dinner with me in the pressroom tonight, and I told you my wife, Julie, had been a car accident."

Ashburn turned to Wheeler with a funny look on his face as the stage manager informed them they had 10 seconds before they would be back on the air.

"Well, how are we going to get out of this one?" Wheeler asked.

"Don't worry pal, I'll handle it," 'Whitey' said.

As they came back on the air, Ashburn went into one of his routines about how brutal the home plate umpire was and then transitioned into his "confession."

"Fans, I'd like to correct something I said on the air last inning. I apparently was given some

"[Houston] is the only town where woman wear insect repellent instead of perfume."

Richie Ashburn

"He looks a little runnerish, Harry."

Richie Ashburn, describing a base runner about to attempt to steal a base

misinformation. Ruly Carpenter was not involved in a car accident today. It was Phillies publicist Larry Shenk's wife, Julie, who was in the accident. We'd like to report that Julie is just fine and that Larry Shenk needs to work on his enunciation."

That night Carpenter was at home, and friends who heard the broadcast started calling him because they were worried about him. He had so many calls that were distracting his

watching of the Vanderbilt–Notre Dame football game that he began hanging up on the concerned callers.

"Vintage Whitey," Wheeler chuckled. "He screws up and then handles it with his wonderful dry humor."

That wit always seemed to surface at the most "appropriate" times. Ashburn made the

A Smokin' Combination: Kalas and Ashburn had a great ability to play off each other on the air.

FRED McKIE COLLECTION

I was fortunate to start with two of the best announcers in the country, By Saam and Bill Campbell. That Saam isn't in the announcers' wing of the Hall of Fame is an injustice that should be rectified. And Campbell still is the best interviewer I've heard in the business.

Harry Kalas replaced Campbell in '71, and when Saam retired in '76, Andy Musser joined the team. Chris Wheeler came along in '77.

Harry probably is my best friend. I say probably, because I don't rank friends, but for as long as I've known him, he always has been there. Being a best friend to Harry Kalas is not an exclusive privilege, I might add. That a lot of folks consider him their best friend is a testimonial to the kind of person he is.

Musser and Wheeler also are very dear friends. In fact, the closeness of the broadcasting team, I think, comes through in the broadcasts. If there is such a thing as a Rock of Gibraltar in the group, it would be Musser. He is the most organized and the most dependable. Wheeler has become the whipping boy of the group, but he takes it good-naturedly, and in truth, I think he enjoys it. "Wheels" easily is the best nonplayer baseball color man in the business.

Richie Ashburn's "My 40 Years a Long Love Affair With Baseball" printed in the Philadelphia Daily News on July 15, 1988

most of every opportunity he had to needle players on the field, members of the Phillies organization, his fellow broadcasters, or even himself.

In 1980, rookie pitcher Bob Walk made quite a splash for the Phillies. Walk replaced Larry Christenson, who was injured, in the starting rotation. During a broadcast of a game pitched by Walk, Ashburn and his broadcasting partner Tim McCarver began a trail of conversation that took them to a place they never expected to go: Mount St. Helens and volcanic ash. As they were discussing Christenson, McCarver mentioned that the recovering pitcher had brought back some ash from Mount St. Helens after a visit back home, and the announcer continued to discuss the descriptive properties of the ash—how the ash from where the explosion had taken place was finer, like dust, while the ash from the other side was coarser. McCarver turned to Ashburn to see his response.

"The kid doesn't chew tobacco, smoke, drink, curse, or chase broads. I don't see how he can possibly make it."

Richie Ashburn

Without batting an eye, Ashburn leaned toward the mike and said, "I think if you've seen one piece of ash, you've seen them all."

McCarver looked at him and couldn't believe that he had made the statement on the air.

So many times during his broadcasting career, Ashburn would take listeners back to his early years in Nebraska. Friends such as Fireball Kelly and Soup Campbell were real people who were important parts of his life.

"Whitey" would regularly entertain the Phillies faithful with stories about his various sports exploits in his early years in Nebraska. If he mentioned his extraordinary ability in baseball, his free throw expertise in basketball, or his claim that he was never once tackled while playing football, you just knew that while he might have laid in on just a little thick, that his stories were all based in truth.

"Richie was Tilden, Nebraska," said *Philadelphia Daily News* columnist Stan Hochman. "He was not a big city guy. His sense of humor stood out. The city loved him so much I think because he had fun doing his job. People appreciated that he had fun and it came through."

Even those within the Phillies organization were able to value Ashburn's personal and unorthodox approach to the mike. Because he was so good at just being himself, his personality was conveyed to all who listened to him, whether it was in person or over the airwaves. It gave them a close connection and access to a ballplayer that not many fans got to experience.

Shenk, the Phillies' vice president of public relations, remembers telling Ashburn about how much he enjoyed getting the autographs of Phillies players as they'd walk across the hallway from the clubhouse to the steps leading to the field at Connie Mack Stadium when he was a child, how he idolized Del Ennis, and how tough it was for him to get to "Whitey" for a signature because he was usually surrounded by six-foot-four pitchers.

"You can bet the house on it. This is a lead-pipe cinch bunting situation."

Richie Ashburn

As Ashburn listened to Shenk reminisce, he looked at the executive and asked why Ennis was Shenk's favorite.

"Because he drove in all the runs," Shenk responded matter-of-factly.

Ashburn took in the answer and replied, "Well, who do you think was on base?"

"There are so many Richie Ashburn stories, and so many people can relate to them because so many people knew him," Shenk posited. "He was broadcasting as if he and Harry were sitting in your living room talking to you. He was so good with people."

"The many-faceted things about his nature made him so appealing to people," McCarver explained. "People get into the habit of listening to an announcer they feel comfortable with. He made it easy to listen to the Phillies as a habit.

what it meant to "look runnerish" and to "freeze a batter." It became part of the vernacular. In backyards and gin mills, when someone boasted that you could bet the house on something, it was Ashburn's influence from the broadcasting booth that made such a bet "a lead-pipe cinch." These phrases were uniquely "Whitey."

In addition to his exceptional way of looking at things, there was also a disarming quality that made Ashburn so popular to so many. Even those who never met him felt like he was a friend.

"The word to describe 'Whitey' is charming," said Phillies president David Montgomery. "He just had an innate ability to charm people. A meet and greet with 'Whitey' was something you'd never forget. He was just gifted. He always made you smile and then turned the smile into a laugh.

"You've got to have a feel for the game."

Richie Ashburn

"Everybody got used to the Ashburnisms. He was a huge influence on how you listen to a game. The one thing I thought he made Philadelphia familiar with was how you played the game."

Not only was "Whitey" known for his personal approach to color commentary with the home-spun yarns about Fireball Kelly and others characters from Tilden, he was remembered for his created phrases that reflected his special knowledge of the game. He used his experiences from the playing field and translated them into terms that became beloved and repeated by Phillies fans. All Philadelphia sports fans knew

"He wasn't bashful, and he framed issues differently from most of us. You just related so well to him. You wanted to hear his stories. Did you hear them before? Yes. Did that matter? No. Listening to 'Whitey' was like enjoying a great song or piece of music.

"He had the ability to humanize the broadcasts. He could bring the listeners right into the booth with him. The pairing with Harry worked so well because of Harry's great gift of describing the action. 'Whitey' put the icing on the cake."

It was impossible for another broadcaster to imitate the Ashburn style. It just wouldn't work

Byrum Fred Saam got this telephone call from Cooperstown, N.Y., a few days ago, and they told him he had been elected to baseball's Hall of Fame. It was a call that has been long overdue. As By's old friend, Willie Mosconi, put it, "It's about bleeping time."

And so it is, and so it finally happened.

Baseball announcers are elected to the Hall of Fame by a committee made up of ex-announcers such as Mel Allen and Ernie Harwell, ex-baseball executive such as Chub Feeney and Bobby Bragan, league presidents Bill White and Bobby Brown, plus baseball writers. To their credit, they finally have recognized the 75-year-old Saam's 38 years of quality broadcasting in the city of Philadelphia. No other major league broadcaster ever worked that many years in the same city.

The committee bypassed Saam in the pecking order for Bob Prince, Jack Buck, Vin Scully and Harry Caray over the last few years. And these announcers are deserving. But not before By Saam.

Saam started working in Philadelphia in 1937, when he broadcast football for the 8-0-1 Villanova Wildcats. It was virtually his last winning season as a broadcaster. In '38 he started with Connie Mack's Philadelphia Athletics and starting in '39, he worked the next 10 years broadcasting home games for the A's and Phillies.

In 1950, when the Phillies added two announcers, Gene Kelly and Bill Brundage, Saam's employer, the N.W. Ayer advertising agency, which owned the radio and television rights to the Phillies and A's, decided Saam should work full time with the A's. That, of course, was the year the Phillies won the National League pennant. ...

Saam did work again for the Phillies after the A's moved to Kansas City in 1955 until he retired following the 1975 season. ...

I had the pleasure and honor of working with By for 12 years. He was a great announcer with a great voice, but most importantly a beautiful man to

CONTINUED ON PAGE 61

All-Star Access: Ashburn's job as a broadcaster allowed him to maintain his friendships with the greats of the game, such as Hank Aaron and Don Drysdale.

unless the same memories and unique perspectives were present. But that doesn't mean that his contemporaries in the broadcasting booth didn't appreciate what he did and how he did it.

"I got a chance to listen to him quite a few times," said former Astros broadcaster Larry Dierker. "He did what I tried to do, but even better. Richie didn't babble on if he had nothing to say. He didn't waste time by making a lot of small talk on the air."

Partners in the Booth

Teamed with veteran announcers By Saam and Bill Campbell, "Whitey" joined the Phillies broadcasting team in 1963. In ensuing years, his broadcast partners included Robin Roberts, Andy Musser, Chris Wheeler, Tim McCarver,

Garry Maddox, Jim Barniak, Mike Schmidt, Kent Tekulve, Jay Johnstone, Todd Kalas, Larry Rosen, and of course, Harry Kalas.

It was hard not to develop a rapport with Ashburn in the broadcasting booth. The dedication and discipline learned between the white lines also served him well in his second career. The many layers of his personality made him an interesting commentator about baseball and life and his approach was observed and learned by the younger broadcasters who joined him in the booth.

"He broke me into broadcasting in a way that only an ex-player can do it," McCarver said. "He would put me on the spot, which helped me learn my responsibility. He had such a unique style. He was incomparable. 'Whitey' loved the game and thought about it uniquely."

"Well boys, I can't be sitting around talking to fans."

Richie Ashburn talking to friends before a game

But Ashburn was more than just a mentor to the men who joined him behind the mike. Because "Whitey" had such a personal technique to broadcasting, he really developed friendships with his partners. Those friendships that began in the broadcasting booth didn't end when the games did, and the traits that endeared Ashburn the player and broadcaster to the fans remained constant when he was off the air.

During their years of broadcasting games together, Musser and "Whitey" became close friends, often car pooling to the games. Musser appreciated Ashburn the ballplayer as well as the broadcaster.

"He was good with people, but he was basically a loner," Musser said. "He liked the road trips. We lived close together and used to car pool. I got to know him real well. He confided a lot to me about family and his career. He was a great family man. He maintained a great relationship and loved all of his kids.

"He was a dear friend. He was older than I was. Sometimes I think that 'Whitey' and I got along better as friends than we did in the booth. But we were good friends. After he passed on, the booth was never the same as far as harmony and camaraderie.

"Every day going to work was like getting together with your buddy."

En route to a long and successful career as a national broadcaster, McCarver teamed with Ashburn as a Phillies announcer. McCarver believed that Ashburn's humor really connected a person to him as a friend and fellow professional. It became the foundation for mutual respect.

"Richie Ashburn, as much as anybody I've ever met, had a relentless sense of humor,"

CONTINUED FROM PAGE 59

work and travel with. He sometimes called innings "rounds" and he always was "rolling along" into the next round, but that was his style, and it worked for 38 years.

Saam worked the games straight and nobody did it better. You were a Hall of Famer long before they made it official.

Richie Ashburn's "Saam's Honor Long Overdue" printed in the *Philadelphia Daily News* on January 25, 1990

McCarver said. "It never ended. The one thing a person like that demands is honesty from the people with whom he is carrying on a conversation. It's what made him so lovable to his friends and the listening audience. That Will Rogers, Richie Ashburn, Tilden, Nebraska-style of humor is very endearing and comforting.

"Richie could cut you to shreds and make you feel comfortable at the same time. I don't think I ever met a person as disarming with his humor. … He could make people feel comfortable. People felt easy around him."

"'Whitey' and I spent a lot of time together," Wheeler said. "He was one of those people who would do anything for you if you had a problem. No matter what, he was one of those guys who would be there for you in a second."

Ashburn also went out of his way to help other members of the Phillies organization. He and misunderstood slugger Dick Allen had a good relationship. One time when Allen left the team during the season in a disagreement with management, it was Ashburn who reached out to Allen to attempt to get him back to the team.

"Richie really won me over when he tried to help Dick Allen," Hochman said. "Allen left the team and missed a game in New York and was then suspended. It was Ashburn who went out to Allen's farm in Perkasie and tried to convince him to come back.

"He liked Allen and kind of understood the rebellious player and got him back. I appreciated the approach Richie took with Dick Allen."

But it wasn't always serious with "Whitey." In fact, most of the memories shared by his fellow broadcasters involved laughter, fun, and games. Whether it was in Florida before spring training or at Ashburn's Clearwater home, the gin rummy games he played with Kirby and/or former teammate Don Zimmer were raucous, irreverent, and addicting.

"We'd go get some dinner and then play [cards] until 2 a.m. or 3 a.m," Kirby recalled. "Many times, he'd beat the devil out of me. Then I'd drive home, and a little while later the phone would ring. In the middle of the night, it was Richie calling to see if I got home okay. He'd tell me that no matter what, he didn't want anything to happen to me. There was a picture of Richie, Pee Wee Reese, and me together. 'Whitey' signed it for me. He wrote something to the effect that two out of three wasn't bad. In other words, two people in the picture were in the Hall of Fame. I wasn't. He was such a great kidder and friend."

"My favorite memory of Richie are those gin rummy games," Zimmer remembered. "He used to make comments all the time. Gene Kirby was older than us, and Richie used to kid him about his age, saying stuff like, 'You ought to be in an old man's home,' 'You can only play with picture cards,' and 'I've got to dummy down to play against you.'

"Gene Kirby and I still get together. Not a night goes by when we don't start talking about Ashburn. And we'll both say, 'Boy, I miss him. He was special to us.'"

That special spirit and wit has been passed down to Ashburn's friends, fans, and family, and when they stop to talk about him, sometimes it is almost as though his dry humor, which made him so popular and beloved, manifests itself in the conversation.

Shortly around the time of Ashburn's death, two other very public figures—Princess Diana of

Home Away From Home: After 12 seasons on the field and 35 years in the booth, the Phillies and their fans were like family to "Whitey."

Wales and Mother Theresa of Calcutta—also passed away. In a good-natured discussion with Richard, Ashburn's son, the subject of what Ashburn's reaction to finding those other two people at the pearly gates of heaven would have been. Richard chuckled to himself and figured his father would take the opportunity to make a joke.

"Boy, I can't even win going into heaven. How can I compete against those two?" he replied with a smile.

The other person returned the smile and then had his own suggestion.

"Or maybe St. Peter would see Richie alongside Princess Diana and Mother Theresa and inquire, 'Who are those two women with "Whitey" Ashburn?'"

"Boys, this Hall of Fame
is screwing up my life."

Richie Ashburn, after being
inducted at Cooperstown

FRED McKIE COLLECTION

CHAPTER FOUR

THE HALL OF FAMER

To those who saw Richie Ashburn play the game of baseball, his impressive offensive statistics are not a surprise. Many remember his blazing speed, his competitive drive, and the joy with which he played the game. For those too young to have seen him, those statistics are more than just impressive. Although numbers can sometimes confuse a situation, his statistics indicate just how good a player he was. Consider how he ranks among fellow Phillies players in the history of the franchise. This two-time batting champion is first in singles with 1,811, second in games played with 1,794, second in at-bats with 7,122, second in hits with 2,217, second in walks with 946, and second in on-base percentage with a remarkable .394. He is third in runs scored with 1,114 and fourth in triples with 97, and he led the league in triples with 14 in 1950 and 13 in 1958.

Trophy Time: Ashburn received many awards during his career, such as the Mets' Most Valuable Player award, but the one honor that eluded him for some time was induction into the Hall of Fame.

Looking at the big picture and how he compared with some contemporaries around Major League Baseball, "Whitey" certainly made his mark and was undeniably one of the best leadoff men of his era. Again, the numbers don't lie.

He led the National League in on-base percentage, in singles, and in walks four times. During his illustrious 15-year career, he boasted a .308 average and was a two-time National League batting champion, hitting .338 in 1955 and .350 in 1958. Two other times, he finished second to Stan Musial. Defensively, he shares the big league record for the most years leading in chances accepted with nine. He still holds the major league record for the most years with 400 or more putouts—nine—and the most years with 500 or more putouts—four.

Ashburn was selected to six National League All-Star teams and was the first Phillies rookie to start an All-Star Game in 1948. He may not have been a power hitter, but he was certainly an iron man, playing in 730 consecutive games between June 7, 1950, and September 26, 1954, the fifth longest streak in National League history. During his 12-year stint with the Phillies, Ashburn played in at least 151 games 10 times and four times played in every game. Between the years of 1949 and 1958, he missed just 22 games.

But perhaps the most impressive statistic of his career is that Ashburn got a hit in 74 percent of the games in which he played. In a typical four-game series, he got hits in three of them. In his own words, he was a "pretty fair country ballplayer."

So although many remember him as the fatherly, neighborly Nebraskan in the broadcasting booth, there can be little doubt that his play-ing career merited induction at Cooperstown. Not only was he an outstanding player in the annals of the Philadelphia Phillies, but Ashburn was also one of the best leadoff-hitting outfielders of his time.

"When I first started playing ball, one of my goals was to get into the Hall of Fame," Willie Mays said. "To me, it was the perfect end to a career. When you go into the Hall of Fame, you are in a group of elite guys. A lot of good ballplayers are not in the Hall of Fame, and you wonder why.

"I always felt with Richie it was just a matter of time. When you hit .340 or .350, you are going to get in. Just because you lead off, you don't have to knock in runs. You have to score runs. One of the problems he might have had is that some guys like me played in the outfield. While we hit .300 and drove in a lot of runs, he was a really good, strong ballplayer too."

Yet, year after year, Ashburn failed to gain entrance to the Hall of Fame. Sometimes it seemed like he would never make it.

"I know he always felt that he had the numbers to get in there," his son Richard said. "But he never really let on. He talked about it more on the air than he did with us. I think he was frustrated mostly with the system, not his being in or not being in."

It is widely accepted that his Hall of Fame selection was delayed because he was unfortunate enough to play during an era of power-hitting outfielders. Three-run homers can often overshadow three-for-four days with three singles.

"I have always felt that the 1950s was the era of the centerfielder," David Montgomery said. "That slowed his getting into the Hall of Fame.

Bat Brothers: Willie Mays and Ashburn faced off for the batting title many times during their careers. Mays always assumed Ashburn would eventually join him in the Hall of Fame.

There are many players who have been overlooked by the Baseball Writers Association of America and are not in the Hall of Fame. And there are many players who are in the Hall of Fame who have been dumped on by the writers. No player ever has been elected unanimously to the Hall of Fame.

In the first Hall of Fame election in 1936, five players—Ty Cobb, Babe Ruth, Honus Wagner, Walter Johnson, and Christy Mathewson—were the first to be immortalized. Of the 226 ballots cast, four writers didn't vote for Ty Cobb and 11 writers refused to put Babe Ruth and Honus Wagner on their ballots.

Eight years later, in 1942, 51 voters out of 233 didn't think Rogers Hornsby was a Hall of Famer. Joe DiMaggio entered the Hall of Fame in 1955 despite the fact that 28 writers didn't put his name on their ballots. And it gets worse. Ted Williams went into the Hall in 1966, 20 votes short of unanimity, and in 1969, Stan Musial didn't measure up to 23 voters.

Wouldn't you think that Willie Mays, Mickey Mantle, and Henry Aaron might find a place on every writer's ballot? No way. Mays was blanked on 23 ballots, Mantle on 43 and Aaron on nine. There is and probably never will be an accounting for some writers' tastes in baseball players.

Rich Ashburn's "Answering Letters on Hall of Fame, Mauch" printed in the *Philadelphia Daily News* on April 21, 1988

You had Mays, Mantle, and Snider all playing out there in a pretty big city just to the north of us. It's very difficult for players whose game did not include power to get early ballot attention for induction."

And no matter how frustrated he might have been with the system or his being left on the outside looking in, that Ashburn sense of humor always surfaced.

"He was frustrated in one sense," Ashburn's oldest daughter, Jean, said. "But in another sense he had a great sense of humor. He always said that he wouldn't belong to a club that would have him. I did not know from him or my mother what a good player he was. It wasn't until I was more grown up that I realized what a good ballplayer he was. But it wasn't like waiting to get in the Hall of Fame weighed him down. He did not obsess about the Hall of Fame; he didn't even obsess about baseball."

The Door Slams Shut

After failing to gain admittance to the Hall of Fame for 15 consecutive years, a player can then only be elected by the Veterans Committee, which can choose two players each year. One year, Ashburn had missed induction by just two votes when two of his Veterans Committee supporters, Stan Musial and Roy Campenella, were ill and unable to vote. Then in 1984, the Veterans Committee selected former St. Louis, Boston, and Washington catcher Rick Ferrell, who hit .281 during his 18-year career. Ferrell had received just three votes from the writers during his years of eligibility. His selection caused some resentment, which in part led to a ruling in 1991 known as the 60 percent rule. The rule stated that except for those players whose careers began before 1946, no player could be considered by the Veterans Committee unless he had been named on 60 percent of the ballots returned in any election.

This amended the previous rule, which made 100 votes in a single year the cutoff. The new rule made it virtually impossible for players such as Phil Rizzuto, Roger Maris, Bill Mazeroski, and Ashburn to ever gain entrance to baseball's hallowed hall.

"In my 15 years of eligibility under the BBWA, my center field opposition consisted of Willie Mays, Duke Snider and Mickey Mantle. Hard to believe I didn't make it against those turkeys."

Richie Ashburn in "Some Writers Belong In Hall of Shame" as printed in the *Philadelphia Daily News* on January 17, 1985

It's not easy to write about yourself, so I'll stand on the record of a .308 lifetime batting average over by 15 years, two batting titles and the holder of some center field putout records that may never be broken. I just finished my 20th year of broadcasting and I am about to start my 10th year of writing for the *Bulletin* and the *Daily News*. And now that the baseball Hall of Fame is inducting broadcasters and writers into their hallowed halls, I stand an excellent chance of being the only man rejected by the Hall of Fame in three different categories.

Richie Ashburn's "The Whiz Kids Baseball, Like The Times, Has Changed" as printed in the *Philadelphia Daily News* on April 5, 1983

The Man with a Plan

After everyone thought that Ashburn's chances for induction in the Hall of Fame were over with the passage of the 60 percent rule, one man appeared in 1991 who made it his goal to change the unfair rule and get "Whitey" into Cooperstown.

Jim Donahue.

A lifelong Phillies fan, Donahue never won a batting title, didn't steal a base, and had nothing to do with any of Ashburn's 2,574 hits. But when Donahue was seven years old, Ashburn signed the youngster's first autograph, a memory that has stayed with Donahue to this day. When he was a child, Donahue's favorite ballplayer was none other than Richie Ashburn. One day before a Phillies game at Connie Mack Stadium, Ashburn took the time to sign seven-year-old Donahue's first autograph.

What was no doubt just a minute out of the day of the Phillies All-Star outfielder, his simple act of kindness and attention was a real life moment for the young boy. His childhood hero took the time to give him an autograph and chat for a minute or so, which made a seven-year-old kid feel like the most important person in the world.

When the Phillies traded Ashburn to the Cubs prior to the 1960 season, Donahue stopped rooting for his hometown team. It was not until Ashburn returned to town as a broadcaster in 1963 that Donahue's loyalties returned to the Phillies.

When it was obvious that someone needed to take the bull by the horn to get Ashburn in the Hall of Fame, it was just as obvious to Donahue that he was the guy to do it.

"When I first spoke to Richie about trying to get the ruling overturned, he said he didn't think that they wanted him in the Hall of Fame," Donahue said. "He was being screwed out of the Hall of Fame but was still the same nice guy I remembered. He was a hero to me then and remained so all those years later.

"Richie was the same guy who would wear tennis shoes with holes in the sides because they were comfortable. He was a terrific guy, friendly to everyone. He treated you like you were special."

Ever the loyal fan who needed to right a wrong inflicted on his boyhood idol, Donahue went to work. He approached Ashburn at an autograph show at the Woodbine Inn in South Jersey in 1991. He asked him if he would mind a grassroots effort to attempt to get the Hall of Fame and to rethink the ruling. Ashburn told Donahue that he felt that the effort would be a waste of time. But No. 1's number-one fan felt that it was his time to waste.

His family understood and supported his countless hours of work on the project. Even his employer helped. But there was a fire in the stomach of Jim Donahue that would not be put

Monday was a black day for Pete Rose. It was the day the baseball Hall of Fame's board of directors ruled unanimously that Rose and all other players banned from the sport cannot be voted into the Hall of Fame.

Had Rose used or pushed cocaine, abused children, or been a roaring drunkard instead of a gambler—keep in mind that $3 billion was waged on the last Super Bowl game—his name could have appeared on the Hall of Fame ballot. Rose might not have been a Hall of Fame husband, manager, or taxpayer, but he was a Hall of Fame player, and that's the last time I'm going to flog that dead horse.

Monday was also a black day for a few other ballplayers, including myself, when the board slipped in another rule that had nothing to do with Pete Rose. Roughly, the rule states that any player, post-World War II, not receiving a best vote total of two-thirds during their 15 years of eligibility will not be eligible for the Hall of Fame, period, end of hopes and dreams.

That ruling immediately ended the Hall of Fame chances of Harvey Kuenn, whose highest percentage was 39, Roger Maris (41), and me (43).

CONTINUED ON PAGE 73

out by anything less than Richie Ashburn being elected to the Hall.

"I saw a rule that was definitely wrong," Donahue said. "I'm just an average sports fan. But I believed Richie belonged in the Hall of Fame and wouldn't give up until he was in. The whole campaign was about getting the rule overturned so that the Veterans Committee could vote him in. That's what it was all about. I thought that other people might agree with me."

Donahue spent countless Sundays and special promotions days at Veterans Stadium during the 1992 and 1993 seasons collecting petitions to have the rule overturned. At the end of the day, he collected more than 165,000 signatures. For a small donation, fans received a "Richie Ashburn Why The Hall Not" bumper sticker. The funds were donated to the ALS; an association that supports research to find a cure for amyotrophic lateral sclerosis, or Lou Gehrig's disease, and a charity championed by the Phillies organization.

With the help of the printing company he worked for, Donahue forwarded 55,000 postcards to the Hall of Fame calling for the rule to be overturned. The postcards read:

"As a fan of Major League Baseball, I feel the current election system for the Veterans

CONTINUED FROM PAGE 71

I can't speak for Kuenn or Maris; they both have passed away. But I suspect they would think it strange, as I do, that a special rule would be passed affecting only three players. The three of us reportedly were strong candidates under the auspices of the Veterans Committee, but that is history, too. Not so incidentally, the rule virtually reduces the Veterans Committee to voting for umpires, managers, major league executives, and a handful of players who survived the post-World War II ruling. Tony Lazzeri, Joe Gordon, Nellie Fox, Gil Hodges, Phil Rizzuto, and Jim Bunning fit into that category. ...

I never have used this column for a self-serving interest, but I am going to register one faint complaint now. The Hall of Fame board of directors consists of 16 members, but of the 12 who showed up for Monday's meeting, only three, Bill White, Bobby Brown, and John McHale, had anything to do with playing baseball. Of the others, Stephen Clark Jr. is the son of the man who donated the land for the Hall of Fame in Cooperstown, N.Y.; Harold Hollis is the mayor of Cooperstown; and Ed Stack is a CPA who administers the Clark family estate.

I can't say if Kuenn, Maris, or I have ever would have been voted into the Hall of Fame. But we should have been given the same consideration every other player has received.

Rich Ashburn's "Rose Not Only One Stung By Hall's Ruling" in the *Philadelphia Daily News* **on February 7, 1991**

Dear Mr. Stack:

As a fan of Major League Baseball, I feel the current election system for the Veterans Committee is extremely unfair. I feel it discriminates against a handful of deserving players, in particular Richie Ashburn. With a .308 lifetime B.A., 2 batting titles and 2,574 lifetime hits, Richie Ashburn certainly deserves further consideration. The "60% Rule" in its present state, has legislated Mr. Ashburn and others from any future consideration. I know the Veterans Committee election procedure is on the agenda of the upcoming annual meeting, and as a fan, I would like my opinion known.

_____   _____
Name   City/State

Printing courtesy of PACKARD

Card-Carrying Supporter: One of the many postcards (left) sent to Ed Stack at the National Baseball Hall of Fame. This one is signed by Philadelphia TV and radio personality Howard Eskin.

Hero Worship: In 1957 Jim Donahue (facing camera and wearing cap) got an autograph from his favorite Phillie Richie Ashburn. Thirty-four years later, that kid returned the favor and led a campaign to get Ashburn in the Hall of Fame.

DONAHUE FAMILY PHOTOGRAPH

The writers rejected me for 15 years. I went from six votes in my first year of eligibility to over 150 votes during my years of eligibility. That's quite a jump, when you consider I didn't make an out or get a hit in those 15 years.

Consolation came only from the quality of support I received from writers for whom I had tremendous respect.

Bill Conlin and Stan Hochman of the *Daily News*, Allen Lewis, the Phillies beat writer from *The Inquirer*, and the late Bus Saidt of *The Times* in Trenton included me on their Hall of Fame ballots.

Pulitzer Prize-winner Red Smith wrote in *The New York Times* a few days before he died, "I voted for Richie Ashburn because he represented 15 seasons of first-class baseball and ungrudging effort." And there was merit to his next sentence, which damned with faint praise: "Ashburn was an outfielder with a better throwing arm than most girls."

I played baseball with only four girls: Myra Mae Hauge, Donnabel Hash, and my sisters, Bette and Donna. I could throw better than Myra Mae, Donnabel, and Bette. But my twin sister, Donna, could not only throw better, she could run faster. Donna could never hit the curveball, though.

Rich Ashburn's "Some Don't Get Honors They Deserve" printed in the *Philadelphia Daily News* on January 4, 1990

Committee is extremely unfair. I feel it discriminates against a handful of deserving players, in particular Richie Ashburn. With a .308 lifetime B.A., 2 batting titles and 2,574 lifetime hits, Richie Ashburn certainly deserves further consideration. The '60% Rule' in its present state, has legislated Mr. Ashburn and others from any future consideration. I know the Veterans Committee election procedure is on the agenda of the upcoming annual meeting, and as a fan, I would like my opinion known."

During the midst of the campaign to get him back on the ballot, Donahue and Ashburn were watching Ashburn's favorite TV show, *Jeopardy*, together. He asked Donahue why it was such a big deal that he be enshrined in Cooperstown.

"I told 'Whitey' that I just knew it was going to happen with Schmitty," Donahue said. "I told him that I was a kid who played baseball but didn't make the high school team. But he had played the next level in high school, in the minors, and then to the majors when there were only 16 teams in the major leagues. Then he became one of the elite players of the game.

"At that point, being 'Whitey,' he said, 'Well, as long as you put it that way, I guess it is a big deal.'"

Although it has never been substantiated just how much the campaign that Donahue led and organized influenced the decision-makers in Cooperstown, in 1994 the rule change that left Ashburn and players of his era ineligible was rescinded. That was the year that Phil Rizzuto was voted in with Ashburn reportedly placing second. And it was only a question of time before Donahue's efforts (and the Veterans Committee) returned the favor.

A Long Time Coming: Ashburn and Donahue celebrate the fruits of their labor in Cooperstown in 1995.

DONAHUE FAMILY PHOTOGRAPH

Finally...

At long last, during spring training on March 7, 1995, as he relaxed in his condo on Harbor Way in Largo, Florida, Ashburn finally got the call. Ed Stack, who was president of the Hall of Fame, gave "His Whiteness" the good news. He and another Phillies great, Mike Schmidt, were going into the Hall of Fame later that summer.

The years of waiting and wondering were finally over. Those who knew him the best understood just how much being a member of the Hall of Fame meant to Richie Ashburn.

"It really bothered him not getting in," Fireball Kelly said. "But he wasn't going to let anybody know it bothered him. After Robin Roberts got in, he felt he had a chance. Finally, when he got in the Hall of Fame, he was very happy. He called me right away. I drove Rich and Herbie up to the Hall of Fame."

Donahue, the man whose grassroots effort had made waves in Philadelphia for Ashburn's induction, was on I-95 driving back from a funeral. Suddenly the radio announced the 1995 Cooperstown inductees—Mike Schmidt by the writers and Leon Day, William Hulbert, Vic Willis, and Richie Ashburn by the Veterans Committee. As soon as Donahue heard Ashburn's name, he began yelling at the top of his lungs and honking the car horn in celebration. To top off the moment, Donahue returned home to a phone message from Ashburn thanking him for his efforts.

At a small intimate dinner party that night in Florida, some of Ashburn's closest friends celebrated the long overdue news with him.

"'Whitey' had a very long day, and he was very emotional that night," fellow broadcaster Chris Wheeler recalled. "It meant a lot to him. It meant a lot for him that his family could enjoy it too."

"I can't believe this great turnout. I was just told that it's the greatest crowd in the history of the Hall of Fame. I wish I could tell you that we had TastyKakes and pretzels out there."

Richie Ashburn

DONAHUE FAMILY PHOTOGRAPH

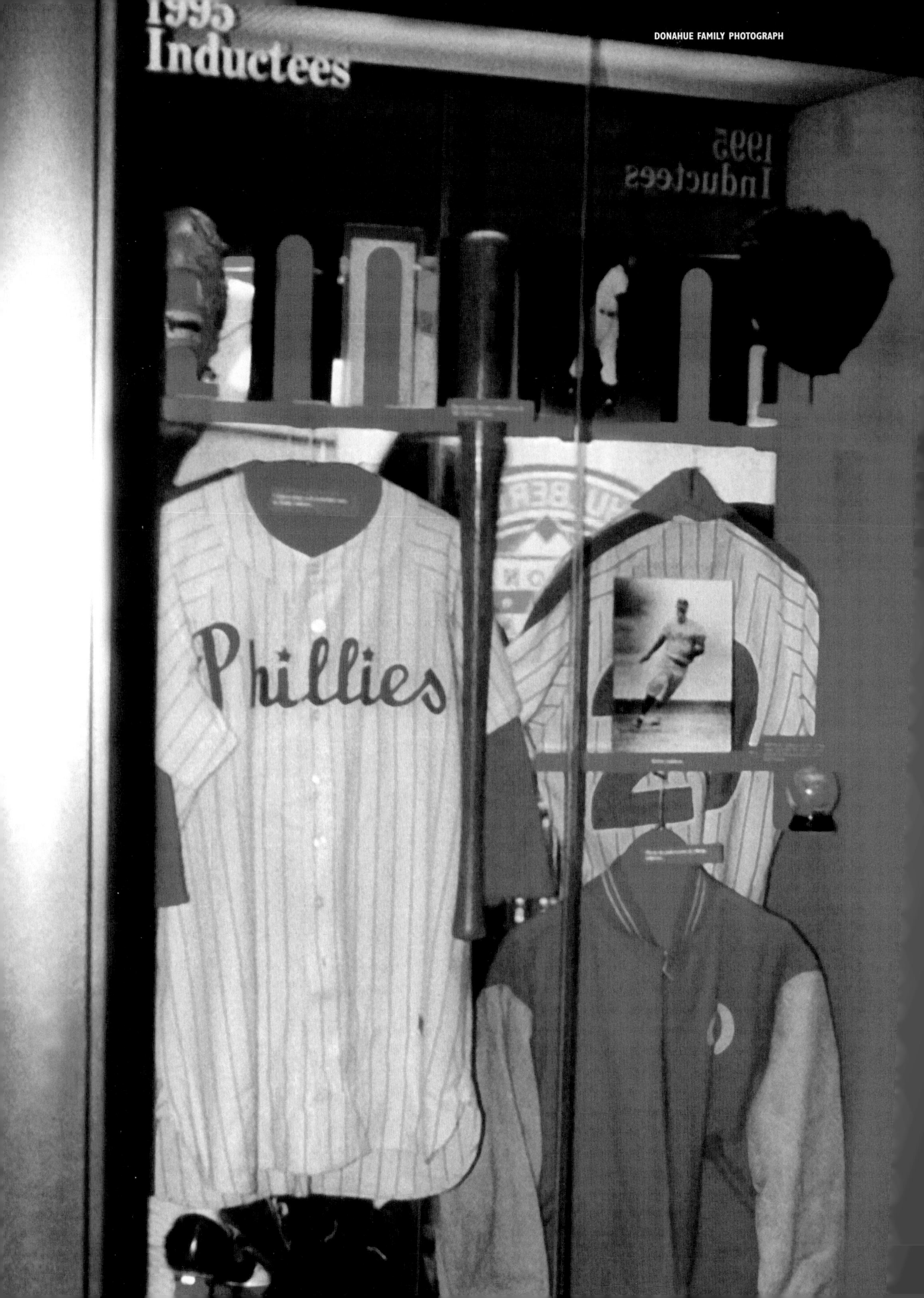

Ashburn's son Richard was driving from Philadelphia to King of Prussia for work when his sister Karen called him to tell him.

"I was so happy for Dad," Richard said. "He belonged there. ...I don't think that Dad really expected to go in at that time and it finally came. It was just amazing.

"I talked to him on the phone that night. It really had started to sink in by then as he had been bombarded with TV and radio. He was overwhelmed, and I had never seen that before.

"I got a kick out of how his life had been turned upside down. That's why he made that joke about the Hall of Fame screwing up his life. He was honored and really happy to go in. But he really enjoyed his quiet life and routine."

It only seemed fitting that Ashburn should share the stage with Schmidt. At the ceremony, the crowds were decked out in red for their two heroes—one who had not had to wait and another who had been waiting decades. The fans had come to appreciate two of Philly's favorite sons.

"'Whitey' and I shared a memorable time together in 1995 when we entered the Hall together," Schmidt said. "They say it still holds the record for Cooperstown attendance. It was a much deserving tribute to Richie and his family. I was overjoyed to share the stage with him."

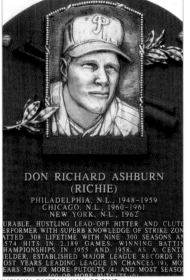

DON RICHARD ASHBURN
(RICHIE)
PHILADELPHIA, N.L., 1948-1959
CHICAGO, N.L., 1960-1961
NEW YORK, N.L., 1962
DURABLE, HUSTLING LEAD-OFF HITTER AND CLUTC
PERFORMER WITH SUPERB KNOWLEDGE OF STRIKE ZON
574 HITS IN 2,189 GAMES. WINNING BATTIN
CHAMPIONSHIPS IN 1955 AND 1958. AS A CENTI
FIELDER, ESTABLISHED MAJOR LEAGUE RECORDS FO
MOST YEARS LEADING LEAGUE IN CHANCES (9), MO
YEARS 500 OR MORE PUTOUTS (4) AND MOST SEASO

NATIONAL BASEBALL HALL OF FAME

Enshrined: Ashburn's locker display was added to the Hall of Fame in 1995 when he was elected by the Veterans Committee.

After years of downplaying the importance of being inducted into the Hall of Fame, those who knew Ashburn realized just how much it meant to him.

"There was complete joy and fulfillment," his wife, Herbie, said. "It was a wonderful day for our family. I've never seen a more popular two players enter the Hall than Mike Schmidt and Rich. It was a fantastic event."

Having two Philadelphia icons inducted on the same day was a once-in-a-lifetime experience for the Phillies organization. It was a special day that will never be forgotten by anyone in attendance or associated with the team.

"One of the highlights of my life was the day that Richie and Schmitty both got in because I adored both of them so much," former Phillies chairman Bill Giles said. "Schmitty for his ability and Richie for his personality. There were nothing but red shirts that day. More people attended that induction than any time before or since. It was real love in a love fest."

More than just a celebration, Ashburn's family and friends said that the ceremony and pomp surrounding it really revealed how important it was to Ashburn to be inducted in the Hall of Fame, despite what he might have said earlier in his life.

"I think the Hall of Fame was very important to him," former teammate and pitcher Bob Miller said. "He always prepared himself for

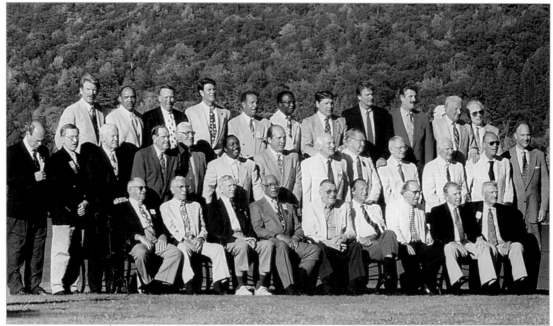

DONAHUE FAMILY PHOTOGRAPH

One of the Gang: Ashburn (top row, far right) joins his fellow members for a photographic moment.

another disappointment as if he wouldn't go in. Like Robin Roberts, 'Whitey' is a Hall of Famer. I know 'Whitey' felt it was the highlight of his life to get in. He was very deserving.

"I think the broadcasting helped people know him. But he was a Hall of Famer because of what he did on the field. Mantle, Mays, and Snider were all in New York. We were 90 miles away. All the hits he got, the longevity he showed, I think what he did on the field got him in the Hall of Fame."

"I think that as a player he deserved to be there," Hall of Fame member Hank Aaron said. "Some guys get in with 500 home runs. He came in with his own credentials that are every bit as impressive as mine. His are just different. That's one of the things that make the Hall of

Fame so special. It's made up of all the different types of players who make up a baseball team."

It was also Richie Ashburn's day, a day that many had waited many years to enjoy. One of the highlights was a wonderful dinner party hosted by Jane Forbes Clark, a longtime member of the National Baseball Hall of Fame board of directors. The food was lavish, and the favors were unbelievable. All of the inductees attended and toward the end of the evening's festivities, they got up to speak. When it was Ashburn's turn, he was not above adding a touch of his humor to the glamorous setting.

"I'd like to be one of the many to thank Jane Clark for this magnificent dinner," he began. "In appreciation for this party, I have one question to ask, 'Jane, why don't you let me take you away from all of this?'"

The room broke out in laughter.

That was the atmosphere of the entire weekend as Ashburn and his family reveled in the accomplishments of his career and the honor finally bestowed upon him.

A Family Affair: The Ashburn family was so excited to share the honor. Here Ashburn's mother Toots (left), and his sister, Bette, survey the festivities.

"It was wonderful," daughter Jean said. "You could see what it meant to him. He was thrilled but also humbled. The day of his induction, that entire weekend, was magical. We missed a lot of the great moments of his career because we were too little. To have it pulled together at the end of his life was a wonderful thing. I was proud of him anyway. But so many other people being proud made it spectacular. It was a Philadelphia day."

It was one of those times when Ashburn was heard to say, "That's only perfect."

Red Letter Day: Phillies favorites Ashburn (left) and Mike Schmidt receive their plaques at the induction ceremony.

CHAPTER FIVE

THE FAMILY MAN

In the fall of 1948, Richie Ashburn was just walking down the stairwell at Norfolk Junior College when he literally bumped into a bright-eyed brunette who he knew was the popular Herberta Cox. That accidental meeting turned into a short conversation, which led to the offer of a first date—a movie.

One date was followed by another to school dances and sporting events, including basketball games in which "Whitey" played. About six months after they met, Herbie and Ashburn were just out on another typical date when out of the blue "Whitey" pulled out a beautiful ring and popped the question. Herbie had no clue it was about to happen.

"We were just out on a date," Herbie said. "I sure was surprised when he asked me to marry him. He had the ring and everything. He was always very thoughtful."

Carrying the Banner: In 2004 the Phillies debuted Ashburn Alley as a tribute to "His Whiteness."

"While my wife was
having six children, I had 13 hits in
27 times at bat, a good run of
hitting in anyone's league. But for
being present at the time of the
births, I was a miserable oh for six."

Richie Ashburn

They married the following year, on November 6, 1949, in Herbie's hometown of Battle Creek, Nebraska. The small service was held at the local Methodist church. Initial plans for a honeymoon in Mexico were changed and the newlyweds went to Omaha, where a lot of their time was spent attending sporting events.

"That didn't bother me a bit," said Herbie with a loving laugh. "I'll never forget his sister Bette saying when we started going out, 'Finally, a girl with some common sense.' We were each other's best friend."

Herbie and Ashburn had a closeness, a camaraderie, and a comfort that was obvious to their friends and in pictures from over the course of their relationship. As a couple, they looked like a natural fit. The friendship, love, and respect that they had for each other superseded any problems or difficulties that occurred.

Becoming a Family

While Ashburn was on the road with the Phillies, Cubs, and Mets, Herbie had six children—Jean

in 1951, Jan in 1954, Sue in 1956, Karen in 1957, Richard in 1959, and John in 1961. Even with the little ones and with her husband out of town, Herbie was able to keep an immaculate house and serve wonderful meals at the dinner table. As the wife of a baseball player, she set up her household—in Tilden and in Philadelphia—and raised her children in an environment that was as normal as she could make it. Through patience, an ability to keep everything in perspective, and a sense of humor that matched her husband's, she built a close-knit loving family that still exists to this day.

"Dad was very clear that he could have never had the career he had without mom," Jean explained. "The two of them worked together. They honored and respected each other as people.

"I remember going through an airport as a little girl with all of my siblings following like chickens and Mom holding a baby. We were all beautifully dressed and very polished looking for little kids. We saw another woman going through the airport with only one child who was attached to a leash. I think that was when I realized what a lady my mom was. My mom was so beautiful and unflappable, very steady. As the oldest, I think I helped her a lot. Jan and I had a game called 'Take the Baby.' When a new baby was born, I'd give her the old baby."

Everyone pitched in and helped, and with Ashburn on the road for half of the year, whether he was in uniform or behind the mike, the chil-

ASHBURN FAMILY COLLECTION

Kids R Us: The Ashburn children at their Nebraska home in November 1963. (left to right) Top row: Jan and Jean. Middle row: Sue and Karen. Front row: Richard and John.

dren never thought their life was all that different from what their friends experienced.

"I don't think they had a master plan," Karen said. "You would learn by their example, and we leaned on each other. We were all very athletic, which kept us all very involved in school. We were just raised to be nice kids. There was nothing special about us. They did raise nice kids, and we all like each other."

That unity and warm spirit was reflected in some of the ground rules Ashburn and Herbie laid down to maintain a good family environment. One thing they required when Ashburn was in town was at least one meal with the

A Real Cut Up: The Ashburn family gathers for a Thanksgiving feast in their Gladwyn, Pennsylvania, home as Ashburn carves the turkey.

Friends Forever: Ashburn gave his wife, Herbie, time off from running the home to relax and play golf, a hobby they both enjoyed.

from his household duties. After an evening of playing with the kids, it was the center fielder's job to run the vacuum. Ashburn even encouraged his wife to take up golf as a hobby, and he gladly took care of the kids so that she could get a break and improve her game.

"I took up golf after having four little girls," she said. "It may have saved my sanity. Rich was very understanding—that I was on overload with kids, especially during the baseball season. He'd be glad to help with the kids when I was learning to play golf."

(Herbie Ashburn is still an excellent golfer today. In fact, she has scored two holes in one in her golfing career, 30 years apart, on the same hole at the same course. And rumor has it that she regularly beat a certain Hall of Fame outfielder on the golf course. It's a rumor she did not dispel.)

"He was a guy who would go out and cut the grass and run the vacuum," Richard recalled. "He was a regular dad with chores and stuff like that. School was very important and sports as well. Dad showed up whenever he could. He missed a lot of things because he was working."

family, even if it was at 3 p.m. before he left for the ballpark.

"Mom and Dad always insisted we have dinner together, no matter what time it was," Jean remembered. "They felt it was more important to have it together than to have it at a certain time. If he was in town, they really tried to have us all sit down at the table together. We all had our jobs to do. But we were each other's best friends."

Herbie ran a tight ship, and even when Ashburn was home, he was not absolved

But even though he wasn't able to attend every game or school production, Ashburn was always the proud papa, boasting about his kids' accomplishments to co-workers and friends at the ballparks. He was even

Hard-Working Man: No matter what the occasion, a party or just playing with the kids, at clean up time, it was Ashburn's job to run the vacuum.

more loving when he was able to be there at his children's performances.

One time Richard was playing in an All-Star Little League game and didn't realize his dad had made it to the park to see him play. His first couple of times at-bat he was able to get on base against a tough pitcher who was really causing his team fits at the plate. But during his last at-bat, the pitcher threw a tricky pitch and Richard popped the ball up.

As he ran toward first, someone in the stands shouted, "You can't hit like your old man."

"Later, I was told that my father waited until the game was over and took the guy aside and really reamed him about treating a kid that shabbily," he said. "He was really mad. He was very protective of all his kids.

"There was never any pressure from him or my family to be like him. To be honest, I'm not sure that anybody could. He never told me what to do. He wanted us to enjoy life, and he did his best to make that happen. We all knew he loved us. Just having him there was a big deal. Dad was definitely a family guy."

And when Ashburn was able to make it, his children remember those moments with fondness. His youngest son, John, thought he was lucky because his birthday—October 4—fell

ASHBURN FAMILY COLLECTION

Daddy's Girls: Ashburn doted on all of his children. Here he is with Jean (left) and Jan.

after most baseball seasons ended, so his dad was there for the celebration.

"He'd take my friends and me to the zoo or play a game he liked called Indian Ball," John recalled. "He loved his kids to death. He never hit or spanked me. If he got angry with you, he'd just squeeze you around the biceps hard."

The end result shows just how effective the effort was that Ashburn and Herbie put into the parenting of their six children.

ASHBURN FAMILY COLLECTION

A Tight Family: The family celebrates Ashburn's 70th birthday in August 1997. From left: Sue, John, Karen, Jean, Richard, Herbie, and Ashburn.

"I remember when Karen used to babysit my daughter," Tim McCarver said. "The way those children all turned out is a testament to and a reflection on the parenting skills of 'Whitey' and Herbie Ashburn."

Take Me out to the Ball Game

Like any family of a ballplayer or baseball broadcaster, baseball was central in the upbringing of the Ashburn children. It determined when their father was home and when he was on the road. It gave them the opportunity to meet some of baseball's biggest names, and it became a way for them to spend time and bond with Ashburn when he was at home.

Every year, as spring training began, the Ashburn family would pack up and head down

to Florida. It held some fond memories for the Ashburn children.

"My parents really did a great job of sheltering us from the public life," Jean said. "But I love baseball and just being at spring training with your family was wonderful and warm. My mom was always happy when my dad was around. You find out later when you get older that it's all about baseball. What's not to love?

"You also feel part of the baseball family, with other families going through the same thing. Behind every professional athlete are a wife and kids who wish he were there more often. We really loved spring training because we were all together."

But their love for the game didn't stop the children from wishing that their father were at home more. Jean remembers hoping every year that her dad wouldn't make the All-Star team

The Next Generation: The Ashburn children at a family gathering in 1995. Pictured from left to right are: (top row) Sue, Jean, Richard (bottom row) John, and Karen.

because that would be three more days with him during the season. It was a wish she kept secret until she filled in for Ashburn as a guest columnist.

"It didn't occur to me as a child that wishing your father would not be on the All-Star team was not necessarily a good thing," she explained. "But it was the life I lived.

"When Dad read that, apparently he got very teary and he told me about it a long time later."

But the Ashburn children were still able to share in their father's love of the game. From the time his kids were little and could hear him on the radio at bedtime, they enjoyed listening to their dad during broadcasts. For at least half of the year, Ashburn was not at home at bedtime, and the radio brought them closer together, no matter where a game was being played.

ASHBURN FAMILY COLLECTION

Proud Papa: Ashburn always let his children know how much he cared for them. Here he is (above) with Sue on her wedding day and (right) sharing a moment with Karen at Christmas.

"I loved to listen to him because I never knew what he was going to say," Richard remembered. "Everything was pulled out of a hat, spur of the moment. It was comforting because I knew he was there. I can remember falling asleep to his games.

"One year when I was older, I did stats in the booth and Dad paid me $10 a game. I stood

behind him and Harry at the Vet. It was so much fun."

His job as one of the voices of the Phillies was also a special experience for his children that gave them access behind the scenes of baseball.

"As a kid, my favorite player was Willie Mays," John said. "The Giants were in town, and I remember walking through the dark corridors of Connie Mack Stadium and then seeing the grass on that beautiful field. Sitting in the dugout were Willie Mays and Willie McCovey. My dad knew them both very well. I got to shake Mays's hand.

"Dad would take us to the games, and we'd go in this old elevator. My brother Richard would tell me that there was a river beneath us and that sometimes the elevator would fall into it. Once I got over that and realized that it wasn't true, it just seemed like we had the run of the place.

"My dad would go to the booth and just to the side was a snack booth, with TastyKakes, burgers, milkshakes. And they were all free. Dad was a great guy, just a normal guy. It was his job to be our dad. We didn't know our life was any

ASHBURN FAMILY COLLECTION

different. It's all we knew. But it was very cool being his son."

That right of passage also allowed the Ashburn children a greater appreciation of their father as a player.

"It was pretty cool for me," Richard explained. "As a kid, I'd go into the clubhouse with Dad and see Tony Taylor, Richie Allen, and Jim Bunning. It was pretty fun."

When Richard was about 11 years old, Ashburn took his son to work down to the ballpark. That day the broadcaster took Richard to the dugout to do an interview with Willie Mays. Ashburn asked some questions and then walked away for a moment. Mays turned to Richard.

"Your dad was the greatest defensive outfielder I ever saw," he said.

Richard sat there in the dugout next to the great ballplayer completely shocked.

Pop Pop is in Town: Richard's son, Taylor (left), at a family gathering with Pop Pop (middle) and Richard's father-in-law, Keith "Hacksaw" Taylor (right).

"To me, Dad was Dad," Richard recalled. "But Willie Mays saying such a thing? I was in awe."

Separate But Still Together

After 28 years of marriage, Herbie and Richie Ashburn separated but never got divorced. So while they came to a point in their union where separation seemed to be the best course of action, they remained unified in their desire to maintain a healthy, loving family environment for their children. It could be said that the friendship between Ashburn and Herbie withstood everything life had to offer.

"I felt it was better for me and the kids to have a happy situation," Herbie said. "He was so grateful for that. I had to work things out that would be the best and healthiest for everyone involved. I was always the practical one, so we complemented each other. He was always good to me and respected me and trusted me."

Despite the unofficial estrangement, Ashburn and Herbie remained close friends

Family Trait: Ashburn's wit and sense of humor have been passed down to his children. Here he and Jean share a laugh at John Ashburn's wedding to Mary Ann Trunks.

Family Friends: Ashburn and Herbie welcomed their lifelong friend Fireball Kelly to spring training in Florida one year.

and worked together to continue raising their family. It was a remarkable testimony to the individual character of "Whitey" and his wife. Holidays were family events at the Ashburn house, with "Whitey" carving the turkey at Thanksgiving and always running the vacuum at the end of the evening—his official duty after collective celebrations. Whatever the family gathering, Ashburn was there with Herbie and the children. And they were so close and such good friends that it was not even the least bit awkward. They would also spend time together in Florida during spring training, where Herbie was a welcomed visitor.

"Rich told me more than once that he'd never divorce Herbie," Fireball Kelly said. "They were still very close."

Although the parting afforded Herbie and Ashburn a more peaceful home environment, it caused a lot of hurt for the children as they adjusted to their father's permanent separate living arrangements.

"When my parents separated, I was unsure of what was going on," Richard said. "I was mad at Dad. But while he was leaving home, he never left us. He was always there. Mom and Dad loved each other from the day they met until the day he died.

"He even said that he loved Mom and always would, but that they couldn't live together right now. You couldn't stay mad at Dad. And he was part of the family all along. I'd still see him a couple of times a week.

"He let us all know he was there for us. He'd do anything for Mom and anything for the family. Even in the darkest of times, they were each other's best friend. He trusted her more than anybody else in his life. Comforting is the word to describe what he was to us."

Surviving a Tragedy

Ten years after Ashburn and Herbie separated, the Ashburn family faced their greatest tragedy. In 1987 Jan, Ashburn and Herbie's second child, was killed when her car struck a telephone pole and the impact broke her neck.

"We don't really know for sure what happened," Herbie explained. "It was very quick, which is something we can accept. I had a premonition that something wasn't right. I spoke with her a few days before and asked her if she was okay.

"It was the last thing we thought would ever happen. I had lost a brother and had learned early that you don't know what is around the

A Lost Daughter: In 1987, Jan (pictured here in grade school) was killed in a car accident. Afterward, friends and family said Ashburn was never the same.

"There is no cure for birth and death, save to enjoy the interval."
—George Santayana, an American philosopher

Jan Ruth Ashburn was born on April 17, 1954, in Tilden, Nebraska, a healthy, beautiful baby girl. I received the happy news at Connie Mack Stadium right after we were rained out of a game against the Pittsburgh Pirates.

Years later, on April 1, 1987, I was in Florida with my two sons, Richard and John, and Richard's wife, Lisa, when I received a message to call Jan at Lankenau Hospital. It was the kind of call all parents with children must dread, but I felt some relief thinking she was able to talk to me.

When I got through to the hospital a distraught nurse mentioned 'a car accident' and 'we did everything possible, but we couldn't bring her back.'

The saddest day of my life grew even sadder when I had to break the news to Jan's mother, Herbie, and her older sister, Jean Meredith, in Louisville and her two younger sisters, SueAnn and Karen Leslie, in Philadelphia.

Harry Kalas shared our family's grief and helped us get through that night. Harry is always there when you need him. Since then, thousands of people, many of whom lost a child, have offered their love and prayers in one way or another. Most of these folks didn't know Jan personally. I would like to thank them for their kindness toward Jan and my family, and for sharing in our loss. For those who didn't know Jan, I want to tell them about her.

Jan will be remembered most for her smile, a smile that brightened every day, every situation. As a little girl with long, flying blond pigtails, I saw her smile after falling down the stairs and losing two of her front teeth. I saw her smile as her head was being stitched while her father almost fainted.

The Rev. John McEllhenney, Jan's minister from the time she was a little girl, quoted poet R.S. Thomas: "... If there are thorns in life, it is she who will press her breast to them and sing. Her words, when she would scold, are too sharp. She is busy after for hours rubbing smiles into the wounds. ... " That was Jan. Rubbing smiles into the wounds.

CONTINUED ON PAGE 97

corner. Living on a farm growing up, I saw life and death every day.

"Rich was in a profession where people protected him and looked after him since he was about four years old. He was in a state of shock. I was, too. But I had to continue to be able to operate through it."

Jan's sudden death shook the family to the core. Every member can recall the pain they felt when they were told what had happened. Ashburn and his two sons, Richard and John, had gone down to Florida for spring training. John, the youngest, was with his father when Ashburn was told about the accident. It had just been an ordinary night—with a father hanging out with his son when the phone rang. Ashburn went in his room to answer the call, and when he returned, he had tears in his eyes and he broke the news to John.

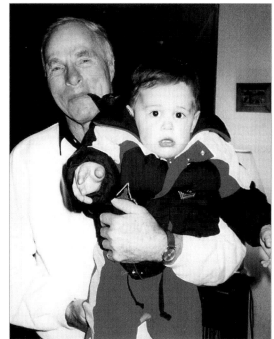

A Proud Pop Pop: Ashburn loved to spend time with his grandkids. Here he is with Karen's son, Sam, in 1989 (above) and with Jean's son, Christian, in 1984 (below).

"How do you console your father?" John remembered thinking. "When my sister died, it was one of the saddest things. And how bad it must have been for Mom. She had to go see her and confirm that it was her daughter. When we flew back home, Mom was emotional, but she was strong as a stone."

Richard and his wife, Lisa, had gone out with Harry Kalas to the dog track that night. It was Richard's first time at the track and so he bet with Kalas most of the night—and lost. On the last race, he decided to pick a different dog from Kalas, and his dog took the race. Richard walked away with around $600, and no one was more ecstatic about his big take than Kalas.

"We're all happy and got back to Largo where Dad had a place, and we found Dad and

ASHBURN FAMILY COLLECTION

ASHBURN FAMILY COLLECTION

The Ashburn grandchildren, Christmas 2004: (from left to right) Neal (kneeling), Taylor (behind chair), Sam (seated), Christian (far back), Jack, John, David, and Harry.

The Ashburn grandchildren, Thanksgiving 2002: (from left to right) Hayley, Sam, MacKenzie, and Jack.

the need to protect her. She was sort of the rebel of the family.

"It's weird. I think that Jan had something to do with that dog winning the race. We found out later from the death certificate that she died at the same time that the dog won the race."

"Rich was a great family man," Andy Musser said. "He maintained a close relationship with Herbie and the children. He loved all of his kids. After Jan was killed, he never fully recovered from that. After that happened, we'd car pool together to the stadium. When we'd got near where it happened, he would become very quiet."

His Legacy

The dedication and love that Ashburn always showed his children has now become evident for the new generation in the family—his grandchildren. Ashburn and Herbie have 10 grandchildren: Neal, Christian, Taylor, Harry, Sam, Hayley, Jack, MacKenzie, David, and John. In his final years Ashburn enjoyed doting on his grandchildren as much as he did his own children. At family events there was always a grandchild on his lap or playing with him.

John crying. They told me what happened. Dad was lost that night. We got on a plane, went back to Philly, and went in to see Jan. Dad had a special relationship with all of us, but he felt

CONTINUED FROM PAGE 94

Rev. McEllhenney didn't know it at the time but he quoted another poet, Dylan Thomas, who just happened to be a favorite of Jan's. "Though lovers be lost, love shall not: And death shall have no domination."

Jan loved the outdoors. A longtime family friend who shared Jan's love of nature, recently wrote, "I walked through the woods—a little girl trudging by my side. A chubby little hand held mine for a feeling of security while stepping stones across a creek. We strode county lanes and talked to birds, of trolls and of trees, and watched a frog."

Jan was a very caring person. She liked to help those who couldn't help themselves. Last winter she asked me if I had some warm clothes for the street people in the city. She knew some of the street people by name and when we put together a huge bag of clothing, she knew just what was needed. "Quentin will get his sweater," she said. "John will like these warm pants."

Two summers ago, Jan was helping some of her friends organize a charity auction for one of her friends whose husband had died in a trucking accident. The tragedy left a widow with three little children. As the day of the auction neared, Jan was worried they didn't have enough items to auction. So she jumped in her car, drove to Atlantic City to the Claridge Hotel and persuaded Mickey Mantle to give her an autographed ball and bat. On the way home, she stopped at Veterans Stadium and got an autographed bat from Mike Schmidt. The three items brought $2,500 at the auction.

Jan loved books. She is the only person I ever saw who could do her household chores with one hand while reading a book in the other hand.

She had a lot of "best friends." At least a dozen people have told me recently, "Jan was my best friend." She found something to like in everyone.

CONTINUED ON PAGE 98

CONTINUED FROM PAGE 97

Jan wasn't perfect. She was stubborn as a jenny mule. Most friends who know me well say Jan came by her stubbornness honestly.

She was very family oriented. She loved her brothers and sisters and they loved her. As all brothers and sisters do, they battled each other occasionally. But if they locked horns, it was because they cared for each other. And if anybody or anything threatened anyone in the family, Jan would have to be reckoned with.

Jan loved plants. The house is filled with plants of all kinds. I have no idea what kind of plants they are or how to take care of them. Some of them she watered, some she took in the shower with her. Because of her love and knowledge of plants, I suggested she get in the business of selling plants. "Dad," she said. "I love them so much I wouldn't want to let them go."

Jan loved baseball, Mike Schmidt and umpire Eric Gregg, in that order. She would have been pleased to know Mike and Donna Schmidt sent beautiful flowers and Eric Gregg got all choked up when he expressed his condolences.

Jan loved and was dearly loved. She would have been 33 years old on Good Friday. Santayana's "interval" was much too short.

Richie Ashburn's "Smile With Me For Jan" as printed in the *Philadelphia Daily News* **on April 28, 1987**

"[My son] Christian and I saw my dad when we lived in Kentucky," Jean said. "It was very easy to get to cities like Cincinnati. One day I left Christian, who was about three, with Dad. Dad gave me a credit card and told me to go out and by myself a birthday present. He'd take care of Christian for me.

"I came back about two hours later and there they were, Dad and Christian, all snuggled up under the covers watching professional wrestling together. Dad said, 'A boy's got to learn how to wrassle.' It's funny because from that moment on my son loved professional wrestling.

"They had a very special relationship. Dad adored all his grandchildren."

In the years following his death, Ashburn's family has done well. Herbie still makes the rounds at the Philadelphia Country Club, has the cleanest house in the tri-state area, and is intimately involved in the lives of her children. The children all have their own lives and have prospered. Jean works for AstraZeneca, Sue is a personal trainer, Karen recently retired from her position at the Pennsylvania Academy of Fine Arts, Richard runs the Rich Ashburn Baseball Academy, and John works as an executive.

"I miss him, having him around," Richard confessed. "He was such a comfort, no matter what the situation. Like when Jan died. There was always a stability about him. Mom has it, too. It didn't matter what was going on, you just felt like it would be okay.

"I miss Dad's stories, his wit. He was such a good guy. He was just Dad to me. I didn't really see how people felt about him until he died. To this day, someone will tell me a story about him every day. He just blew

people away. And he didn't even know he was doing it."

His legacy and the love his fans had for him resonated with the Ashburn children and helped put in perspective just what kind of man and how much of a beloved son he was to the Philadelphia area.

"It's almost impossible to listen to a game and not long to hear Dad there," Karen recalled. "I miss him all the time. I miss him for my kids more than anything—that they really don't know what a riot he was.

"He loved his family. He was the most respectful person I ever met, and he taught us to be respectful. For each of us, he was a different dad. He meant everything to us.

"At Memorial Hall, whatever the total number of people went there, I knew only two people in the lines. I thought, wow, I only know two of this great number of people. What a great, great honor to be his daughter. For all of those people to show up and want to say goodbye."

The family speaks of a symmetry that they felt between the happy occasion of Richie Ashburn's induction into the Hall of Fame and the sad occasion of the public service following his death that was held at Memorial Hall. At Cooperstown, they could see people dressed in red and white seemingly to the horizon and beyond. Two years later at Memorial Hall, people, wishing to pay their respects to the family, were waiting in line as far as the eye could see.

On that sad day in Philadelphia, Ashburn's family did exactly what they knew he would have done in a similar circumstance. They stayed and greeted every person who waited in line to pay their respects. It is the Ashburn way.

AFTERWORD

Time heals all wounds, and we all have the ability to move on and bounce back. The death of a family member, loved one, or a close friend can be a traumatic experience that is difficult to overcome. When Richie Ashburn passed away in September 1997, he left a family, friends, associates, and millions of fans who were touched not only by his passing, but by his life.

This tribute to Richie was not to make him into something he wasn't or to immortalize him as more than he was. In truth, he was just a man. But he was a man who had a lot of ability. He was a Hall of Fame baseball player, an outstanding broadcaster, and a talented writer who could share the most serious personal thoughts or just kid around. He gave the impression that he was everyman, but in truth he was a rare quality of a man.

Why was he so popular? What made him a virtual untouchable as far as criticism was concerned in such a critical city?

A person could talk for hours about what made Richie Ashburn special. But as his daughter Jean stated, he was very comfortable in his own skin. He knew who he was and felt comfortable with himself. That self-confidence and his ability to not take himself or everything in life all that seriously made him a joy to be around. No matter what the situation was during a ball game, there would always be the "Whitey"-esque way of looking at things. There was always a story or a name from his early days in Nebraska to make the story complete.

From hearing some of the tall tales as well as some of the touching personal stories, it became

Remembering Richie: Phillies broadcasters Tim McCarver (left), Harry Kalas (middle), and Ashburn (right).

> "The one thing I admired most about 'Whitey' was his individuality. He truly was his own man. His dress, his stance, his golf swing, his gin game, his comments, and his sense of humor were all pure 'Whitey.' I would have given anything to have eased through life with his carefree attitude."

Mike Schmidt

evident that Richie Ashburn was just always Richie Ashburn.

He was a charmer, with great wit and unique perspectives. He was a product of his Nebraska roots, which shaped his outlook on the world as well as his outlook on daily life. "His Whiteness," as Harry Kalas would call him, simply had the complicated ability to make people feel better about life in general and themselves in particular.

It's fitting that Richie Ashburn wore No. 1 during his brilliant playing career, because he was first in the hearts of Philadelphians, and he was absolutely one of a kind.

The mourning over his death was very much like losing a member of the family. Gone are the funny stories and the signature hat and the pipe. There are no more birthdays, anniversaries, and get wells to be delivered between pitches.

But rather than enjoying Ashburn Alley or reading an account such as this and feeling sorry for our loss, let's remember "Whitey" as "Harry the K" does, with a smile on our faces and warmth in our hearts.

For as much as it hurt to lose him, knowing him, seeing him, and hearing him for so many years was worth the pain.

I couldn't think of a better way to honor his memory.

—Fran Zimniuch

CAREER STATS

CAREER STATS

Year	Team	AVG	G	AB	R	H
1948	Phi	.333	117	463	78	154
1949	Phi	.284	154	662*	84	188
1950	Phi	.303	151	594	84	180
1951	Phi	.344	154	643	92	221*
1952	Phi	.282	154*	613	93	173
1953	Phi	.330	156	622	110	205*
1954	Phi	.313	153	559	111	175
1955	Phi	.338*	140	533	91	180
1956	Phi	.303	154*	628	94	190
1957	Phi	.297	156	626	93	186
1958	Phi	.350*	152	615	98	215*
1959	Phi	.266	153	564	86	150
1960	Chi	.291	151	547	99	159
1961	Chi	.257	109	307	49	79
1962	NYM	.306	135	389	60	119
Total		**.308**	**2,189**	**8,365**	**1,322**	**2,574**

*Led League

Richie Ashburn

Batted: Left

Threw: Right

Height: 5' 10"

Weight: 175 lbs.

2B	3B	HR	RBI	BB	SB	SLG
17	4	2	40	60	32*	.400
18	11	1	37	58	9	.349
25	14*	2	41	63	14	.402
31	5	4	63	50	29	.426
31	6	1	42	75	16	.357
25	9	2	57	61	14	.408
16	8	1	41	125*	11	.376
32	9	3	42	105	12	.448
26	8	3	50	79	10	.384
26	8	0	33	94*	13	.364
24	13*	2	33	97*	30	.441
16	2	1	20	79	9	.307
16	5	0	40	116*	16	.338
7	4	0	19	55	7	.306
7	3	7	28	81	12	.393
317	109	**29**	586	**1,198**	234	**.382**

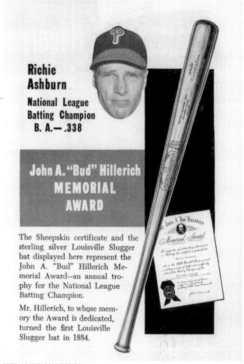

Richie Ashburn
National League
Batting Champion
B. A.— .338

John A. "Bud" Hillerich MEMORIAL AWARD

The Sheepskin certificate and the sterling silver Louisville Slugger bat displayed here represent the John A. "Bud" Hillerich Memorial Award—an annual trophy for the National League Batting Champion.

Mr. Hillerich, to whose memory the Award is dedicated, turned the first Louisville Slugger bat in 1884.

FRED McKIE COLLECTION

Phillies

50c

ROBIN ROBERTS
Leading Pitcher in Major Leagues
1955

1956

RICHIE ASHBURN
National League Batting Champion
1955

WORLD SERIES 1950 VERSUS NEW YORK YANKEES

Year	Team	AVG	G	AB	R	H	2B	3B	HR	RBI	BB	SB
1950	Phi	.176	4	17	0	3	1	0	0	1	0	0

ALL-STAR GAMES

Year	AVG	G	AB	R	H	2B	3B	HR	RBI	BB	SB
1948	.500	1	4	1	2	0	0	0	0	0	1
1951	.500	1	4	2	2	1	0	0	0	1	0
1953	1.000	1	1	0	1	0	0	0	1	0	0
1958	Did not play										
1962	1.000	1	1	1	1	0	0	0	0	0	0
Total	.600	4	10	4	6	1	0	0	1	1	1

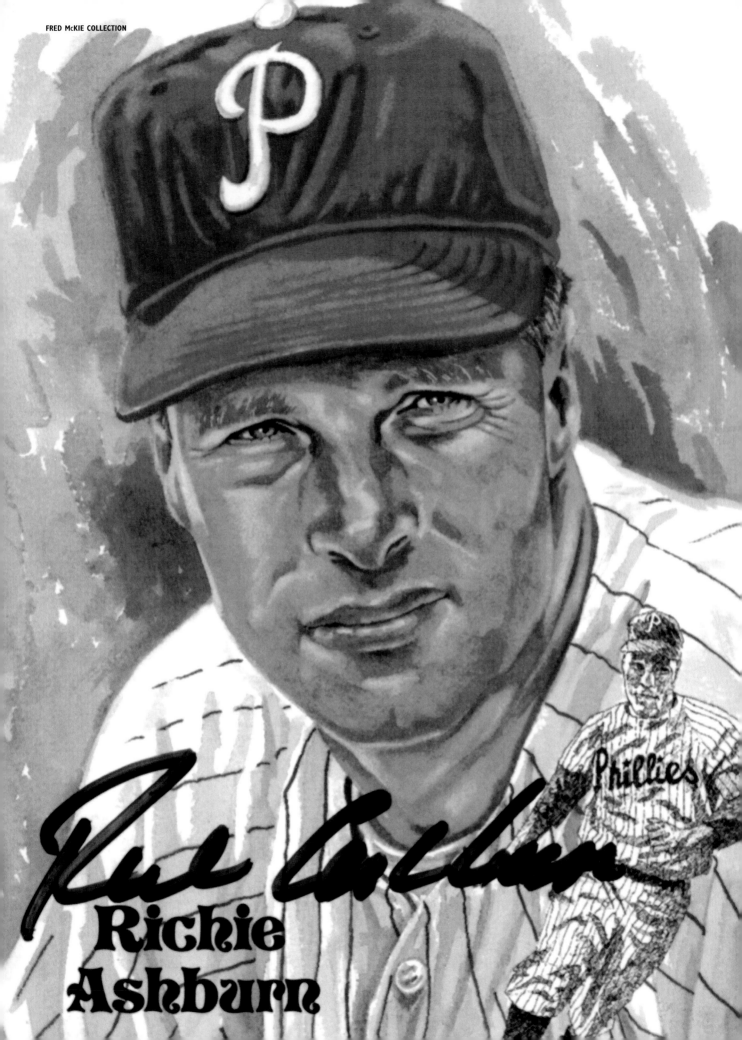

Richie
Ashburn

THE RICHIE ASHBURN
BASEBALL FOUNDATION

For the past 50 years the name Richie Ashburn has been synonymous with Philadelphia baseball. His love for the game was matched only by his love of watching kids learn and play the game. His love of children is evident in the quote above which was passed on to all Philadelphians in Phillies broadcaster Harry Kalas's eulogy of my father. Dad's dream was to help and influence in a positive way as many kids as possible. Thus, the Richie Ashburn Baseball Foundation, a registered 501 (c)(3) charitable organization, was founded to carry on his dream.

The Richie Ashburn Baseball Foundation, founded in 1998 by Rich Ashburn Jr.; William Penn Charter School's baseball coach Rick Mellor; and Philadelphia Phillies assistant general manager Ruben Amaro Jr., is dedicated to helping kids in the city and surrounding communities. Our goal is to provide children in the city and suburbs the opportunity to learn baseball by offering free camps throughout the area. Using the game as a teaching tool, we touch on the more valuable lessons in life, such as sportsmanship, drug and alcohol awareness, and the importance of a quality academic education. The foundation also helps to find academic grants to local private schools.

The Teacher: Ashburn shares some words of wisdom to Phillies players at spring training.

My father's dream of helping kids will live on through me. In order to continue this dream, we need your help. Dad strived to bring Philadelphia's corporate, civic and political leaders together for the sake of our youth. He believed that our community leaders, along with major league players and coaches, are role models for the future success of our children.

In recent years our program has grown from five coed baseball camps serving 350 kids with two academic grants to 23 camps and clinics for over 1,250 kids and a third academic grant. We look to the future with the hope of adding more camps and clinics, plus additional academic grants. The foundation is also looking forward to its first Richie Ashburn Baseball Classic for players ages 13 and under. I know my father would be proud of anyone helping this cause.

Sincerely,

Rich Ashburn Jr.

AP/WWP

For the Love of the Game: Part of Ashburn's legacy is to share the love "Whitey" had for the game with the local Philadelphia community.

"If you can make a difference in the life of just one child, then his memory will be fulfilled."

Harry Kalas